UP TO SOMETHING BIG

STORIES THAT INSPIRE CHANGE

First Printing: January 2012

ISBN: 978-1468098860

Cover and book design by Leisha Tanner, www.digitaltractordesign.com

Printed on recycled paper in the United States of America

For more information about this book or the author, please visit:

www.daviarivka.com

UP TO
SOMETHING
BIG

STORIES THAT
INSPIRE CHANGE

by

Davia Rivka

CAR.   2·2·12

Thank you, Thank you
for being big in my life.

Davia

ACKNOWLEDGMENTS

The seed for this book was planted during the long year that both my daughters left for college and my husband left our marriage—a time when I learned a lot about being up to something bigger than myself. I am grateful to so many wise teachers whose books and stories carried me through that time, starting with Rachel Naomi Remen, whose book *Kitchen Table Wisdom* felt like a child's night-light in my darkness. Pema Chödrön let me see the gifts that come when things fall apart, and David Whyte reminded me how to listen for my own voice. It was my coach, Tracey Trottenberg, who gently and intentionally coaxed this book out of me after the idea lay dormant for ten years. Thank you to my friend, coach, colleague, Colleen Bracken, who reminded me who I was when I forgot.

Thanks to my many clients, particularly the ones who gave me permission to retell their stories here. To preserve their anonymity I have changed the details of their lives, but what you read here is true to the core challenge each faced. Their willingness to step into the unknown has been a constant inspiration to me.

My life as a writer began shortly after my fiftieth birthday. I want to express my deep appreciation for all my teachers, who encouraged me as they held the bar high: Melisa Cahnmann-Taylor, Toni Brown, Nava EtShalom, Stacie Chaiken, and Jack Grapes. Thank you also to all in the Wednesday morning class that is my community of writers. That class anchors my writing days and reminds me to get out of my own way and put pen to paper.

Initially, I didn't know what story I was trying to tell, and several editors helped me at different stages. Donna Frazier took in my jumble of words, asked the right questions, and made spot-on suggestions so that the statue could emerge from the stone. Robin Rauzi cleaned it up and made it flow. Her craft is there, woven elegantly between the lines. Karen Chaderjian gave the attention to fine details that leaves the eye satisfied.

Thank you to Leisha Tanner for her design eye and willingness to put up with my extensive input on the book's cover.

In between long hours of writing, I have been a secondary caregiver for both my parents. And I haven't been alone. Thank you to my sisters—Jan Burns, Eliana Berlfein, and Judy Berlfein—for their willingness to tackle difficult conversations, hard decisions, and heartbreaking changes. They also have made this book possible.

A desire to heal the places that are broken in the world seems to be embedded in my DNA, and for that I must also acknowledge my mom and dad, Jean and Hal Berlfein, who weaned me on the value of giving back.

True to my own words, I keep myself surrounded by people up to something bigger than themselves, who remind me what I'm up to when I forget. That makes all the difference.

Thank you.

CONTENTS

INTRODUCTION

People want their lives to matter. They are hungry to leave the world a better place than they found it. They passionately want to make a difference, but don't always know where to begin, how to stay focused, or what to do when challenges seem insurmountable.

As a life/work coach, I've listened to stories from hundreds of clients—executive directors, community activists, entrepreneurs, artists—about how eager they are to live lives that matter. These are ambitious people with vision for whom giving back is a central value; they are eager to find ways to maximize their contribution. As they go out into the world, however, sometimes they undermine their own best interests, or get derailed by their blind spots. In our work together, I give them tools and practices to build strength from the inside, so that they may accomplish their goals on the outside.

Of course, we teach what we most need to learn. It was my own desire to live a life that mattered that set me on this path. Twenty-five years ago, I began speaking to members of Congress on behalf of impoverished women in developing nations. As I gave voice to their needs I was surprised to discover how difficult it was for me to speak up. Willingness and practice propelled me forward into greater advocacy, a coaching career, and now into writing this book.

I know firsthand how the journey of change begins from within, and this forms the foundation of my work with all my clients. Coaching helps them close the gap between their vision for the world and their behavior toward themselves (or those close to them). This behavioral discrepancy is not hypocrisy—more just an unobserved misalignment that I help them see and repair. For instance, I have worked with organizations committed to global sustainability where, in direct contradiction to their visionary goals, the staff are saddled with unsustainable workloads. I've worked with organizations committed to community collaboration whose internal staff are at odds with one another, their backbiting behavior undermining any progress. I have seen high achievers with full CVs who lacked confidence, visionaries who couldn't incorporate others in their vision, and leaders who struggled to communicate clearly and cleanly.

What does it mean then to make a difference from the inside out? Think of it as preparing to climb a mountain. You want to reach that summit—but before setting foot on that mountain, you train. You run, walk, climb, eat right, sleep well, get the right gear. You prepare yourself to successfully make the ascent. The training doesn't make the mountain less steep or the accomplishment less meaningful, but your relationship to the climb changes. You don't have to fight your way up, but instead move forward and upward with ease and grace—even as you encounter rocky terrain.

This book is a collection of stories about people who are developing the skills and practices that will get them to the top of a mountain. In the words of Gandhi, they are striving to "be the change you wish to see in the world."

Clients come to me envisioning big change in the world. How do they embody that change? They have messy, complicated lives. None has transcended fear, sadness, or anger. They are human. They long to connect with people and find meaning in their work.

As I coach them, their vision guides them forward, amplifying behaviors and actions that need attention. I watch my clients release confining ideas, try on new habits, and push themselves physically, mentally, emotionally, and spiritually—sometimes past the edge of their comfort. In the process of healing themselves, they heal those around them. Their newfound (or renewed) abilities extend outward in ever-expanding circles: neighborhood, community, state, national, global.

It is a journey for the courageous. Some weeks they stumble. But some weeks all the planets line up and they are energized by their own movement.

I hope you, too, will be energized as you read their stories. I know that in my own life, I have taken comfort and inspiration from the stories of those who have come up against hard spots, and pushed through them, creating more light and space in their lives in the process. Those stories were a path for me—rarely linear, often circuitous—through some of the most chaotic and messy stages of my life. They were the markers that led me through.

On hiking trails, those who've walked the path

previously stack rocks into a cairn to mark the way forward when it's not clear. This book is my rock cairn, each stone a lesson of personal growth from people who are up to something big.

Chapter One

Develop Practices

The summit of Mount Everest is 29,035 feet above sea level. Mountaineers train rigorously before making an ascent. Conditions are extreme and unpredictable: Oxygen is thin, temperatures are well below zero, and avalanches are a constant threat. Endurance, stamina, and mental preparedness can mean the difference between life and death.

Most of us are not climbing Mount Everest. But we do face the rigors and unpredictability of our own journey. Without strength and support we can easily get blown off course, betray our values, or forget where we were headed.

Support can be generated from the outside, but strength grows from the inside, every day. To build it, put practices in place to exercise the wisdom of body, mind, and spirit. Develop discipline, honor commitments, and stay focused.

A daily practice fortifies our core; it builds us from

the inside out. This is the "day after day, unglamorous scales on the piano, push-ups on the field, writing one sentence after another" part. It is "the ugh, not again, I don't feel like it" part.

And yet it is here in the practices that vital muscles get built. The muscles of consistency, of accountability, of reverence. It is this daily, brick-by-brick attention to detail that builds the cathedral.

MY LESSON

The Body Is Precious

The only way to get my attention sometimes is to hit me over the head—or bite my back. I was fifty years old and had been ignoring my body. Taking my limbs and mind for granted. I was eating too much sugar and wasn't exercising. I had stopped meditating. Until one hot summer day, sitting in my backyard, something bit me in the middle of my lower back. The bite started out the size of a nickel and was surrounded by a red halo. A week later, it had spread over both sides of my back and met at my belly button. The halo grew with it. My arms collapsed under me when I tried to hoist myself out of a swimming hole. I put it down to the heat. Everything made me cry.

Doctor after doctor failed to identify the bite. Six weeks later I ended up in the emergency room in agonizing pain. The emergency room doctor recognized it right away; lyme disease. Six weeks of pain. Six weeks of mental disorientation. The antibiotics kicked in, and the excruciating pain began to subside, but it took a nine-month regimen of antibiotics before my body was fully recovered. I felt battered, my aching body an immense weight. Lifting, sitting, standing, thinking, demanded extreme effort.

I know my body needs food, water, exercise, and sleep.

But there is often a gap between what I know and what I do when I get up. Lyme disease upped the ante. Here are your options, it shouted: Eat well, sleep well, exercise, and meditate—or you won't have a body that can carry you out into the world. Pain forced me to pay attention.

My body became precious. I needed it to make it through a day without collapsing. I needed my brain to be able to hold on to a thought and move it forward.

As soon as I regained an ounce of strength, I returned to yoga. I went to class three times a week, and I did my own practice at home on the other four days. I was like a thirsty wanderer in the desert. Yoga was my water. Still, I moved very slowly. Sometimes I would just lie on the mat, unable to gather myself into a pose. While the antibiotics fought off the lyme, they also chased out the good bacteria in my system, leaving me feeling depleted. Eating right became a sacred ritual. Every aspect of feeding myself filled me with gratitude. It anchored my days. Sleep was fundamental. I started meditating again. And journaling.

I rebuilt the foundation of my health, the structure that held me. I never loved my body so much. Lyme taught me: Build your body strong. Build it healthy. Build discipline. Build dogged commitment to one day, one day, one day. Tend to yourself.

I relearn the lyme lesson over and over. I remember my body, exercise it, feed it well, sleep it, meditate it. Then I forget. I start to assume that I will have my arms and legs, my energy, my clear thinking. Until another Lyme lesson reminds me, sometimes loudly, sometimes quietly.

HANNAH

Bedtime

"The houses aren't getting built fast enough, we don't have enough volunteers, we don't have enough money, the city won't give us permits, the families aren't putting in their sweat equity." Hannah exhales the words in one long, run-on sentence.

She is the director of a small nonprofit with a big mission: collaborating with low-income families to build their own houses, creating a base from which they can step solidly into the world. Hannah is a rocket—five feet tall with a shock of short blond hair and large red-framed glasses—and ready to blast off at any minute. She would make a great backcountry expedition guide, high-spirited, ready to take on lions and tigers and bears. Her job is big. She is responsible for raising money, hiring and firing staff, recruiting volunteers, training new homeowners, and collaborating with other community organizations.

"I can't hold it all," Hannah says. "When I pick up one thing I drop another. I manage ten paid staff and fifty volunteers. There's always some crisis that needs my immediate attention and there I am, a day late and a dollar short."

I can feel all those tasks frenetically flying at her. She is like a kite gone wild in the wind, tethered to nothing.

"Hannah, I'm going to tell you what I heard you say. Sometimes just hearing your own words gives you a different perspective. You said the houses aren't getting built fast enough, you don't have enough volunteers, you don't have enough money, the city won't give you permits, and the families aren't putting in their sweat equity. You said you can't hold it all. When you pick up one thing, you drop another. You manage ten paid staff and fifty volunteers. There's always some crisis that needs your immediate attention and there you are, a day late and a dollar short," I say.

We are at the organization's headquarters, an old, gutted warehouse with temporary plywood walls. Hannah's office is a desk in the corner, a broken chair held together with duct tape leans against it. A makeshift wall separates her visually from the rest of the open space. Just beyond her desk, wood sawhorses are stacked and a project timeline is tacked to the wall. There are splats of drywall compound on the concrete floor. A torn Mr. Goodbar wrapper from yesterday's lunch sits on the desk.

"You got it," she says. "What a mess. And when you say it, it sounds even worse than when I say it."

"What I notice right away, is that you can no longer think clearly or creatively. You're all filled up. There's no room for anything else. Before you can address anything—the houses, the volunteers, the money, the permits, the families—you need to create some quiet space deep inside of yourself. Does that make sense?" I ask.

"Well, sure, it sounds great, but how the hell do I do

that?" she says. "I mean, of course that's what I need to do, but I'm just spinning in circles. I don't know how to stop spinning."

"You're in the business of building houses. You tell me, what makes a house sturdy and solid? What gives it longevity?" I ask.

"Easy. It needs a good foundation. It needs a good frame. You have to use high-quality materials. And there needs to be integrity in the workmanship. No brainer," she says.

"Let's apply the same rules to you as a human being!" I say. "Let's talk about your foundation, your frame, the materials you're using, and the integrity of your workmanship. OK, so maybe I'm taking the analogy too far. But I think you get the picture."

She is batting a pencil back and forth across the desk. It is late in the evening and we are the only ones still in the warehouse. All the tools have been put away for the night and the floor has been swept. I know that it is not usually this quiet, and I wonder how Hannah can get anything done amid so much distracting activity.

"Let's start really basic," I say. "Talk to me about your sleep habits."

"Whoa, I didn't hire you to talk about when to go to bed!" she replies. "I have a big job to do here. Sleep may be a luxury that I have to forgo at times to get the job done."

"That's true—at times you may have to work long hours. But let's take a look at what you are doing now. Think of it like exploring. We'll collect the information and then you can make some choices once you have all the data," I say. "What do you know about your sleep habits?"

"I'm bone tired. All the time. I know I don't get enough sleep, but when I get home from work I'm all wound up so I figure I'll just sit at my computer and read my e-mail and play solitaire to try to unwind. But it has the opposite effect; it just keeps me on low-grade hyper-speed. And before I know it, it's 1 or 2 in the morning," she says.

Hannah is still rolling the pencil back and forth.

"I have noticed that 10:30 is my pumpkin hour. If I stay up past 10:30, forget it! I don't end up going to bed until 1 or 2," she says. "Then I don't sleep well, and I'm not so good the next day. Too many times I come to work late, and that certainly doesn't set a good example. If I could get myself to bed by 10:30, I think it would be miraculous."

She's asking herself for a bedtime. Structure. A practice. "When my kids were small, I used to start the bedtime process about forty-five minutes before their actual bedtime," I tell her. "We had a long wind-down, get-ready-for-bed ritual. They put away their toys, put on their pajamas, complained about going to bed, brushed their teeth, complained some more about going to bed, asked for a glass of water, and finally got into bed. I read them stories until they both fell asleep.

"If you want to be in bed, ready for sleep by 10:30, start to think about your get-ready-for-bed-ritual. Think about how long you'll give yourself for the wind-down, what your wind-down activities will be," I say.

She stops playing with the pencil and looks up.

"Wow, I can't believe that I've never even considered these things before. They make so much sense. For starters, the computer cannot be part of my wind-down process. It does not calm me down. Maybe if I listened to classical music. I love it but never seem to have the time to listen," she says.

"Another suggestion: For this week, keep track of what time you go to bed. And any other notes that will help you make choices about how to make the bedtime thing work for you," I say.

The next week she gives me her bedtime report. "Ugh, one night 10:30, two nights 11:30, the rest around 1:30. Ugh. This is hard. I got seduced by solitaire on the computer, and one thing led to another and it got late. It was easier before we started this conversation. I just went to bed too late and didn't think about it. Now I know I'm a loser," she says with a twinge of a smile.

"You're doing great," I tell her. "I know it seems like it should be easy. After all, you're a grown-up, you should be able to go to bed at a time that works for you. If it's any consolation, this is where many of my coaching sessions start! We start with the basics. Because, as you know, if the house isn't sitting on a strong foundation, if the workmanship is faulty, that house isn't going to last for very long. The same goes for you. Your physical well-being makes a big difference in the way you show up for work. It seems that the simple things are the hardest. Once you get this down, your job will start to look like a piece of cake," I say. "What worked the night you went to bed at 10:30?"

"Well, I got home around 9, listened to some classical

music, started getting ready for bed at 9:30 and felt quite relaxed by 10:30. I fell asleep easily and had a great night's sleep. Wow, bravo for me!" she says.

"How about if your goal for this week is to be in bed by 10:30 three out of seven nights?" I ask.

She slaps her hand on the desk. "I'm there!" she says with a big grin.

"Here's what we're looking for. Begin to notice how a good night's sleep impacts your work."

Four weeks into her experiment, she begins to look and feel rested. "Something amazing just happened," she says. "Richard slammed his hand down on my desk and started ranting about how he can't trust Michael with a project. I listened to him without wanting to jump down his throat. I was calm, and my even voice calmed him down. We had a good chat, and we have a plan of action. This is not how I usually respond. I'm always fast to fly off the handle. Richard was a little shocked by my reaction. Pleased, but shocked," she says.

The next time I come to see Hannah at her office, she has cleaned up and rearranged the space. She's moved her desk to the opposite wall, filed her papers, updated the project timeline and put up another piece of plywood to create more privacy.

"When you first called me, you said you couldn't hold it all, that when you picked up one thing, you dropped another. We've just spent several weeks retraining your sleep habits. We're just beginning our foundation building work, but let's pause here. Tell me what you notice at this point," I say.

"It's not perfect, but I feel like I'm beginning to think more clearly. I don't flip out when staff dumps something on me. In fact, I can even notice that maybe they're not getting enough sleep or something else basic like that. Ironically, I feel like I have more time! That seems like it's a contradiction, but I actually feel like something has been taken off my plate. I suspect I know what we're going to talk about next—food and exercise!" she says.

When Hannah and I began to work together, I expected we would focus on issues related to running a nonprofit. But the nonprofit's work rested on Hannah's foundation, and we had to start there. There was a lack of congruency between her leadership and the mission of her organization: building foundations (houses) for families, providing platforms for sustainable lives. As she began to put her own house in order, Hannah brought clearer, more solid leadership to the mission. The bedtime issue, which initially seemed trivial, revealed itself to be fundamental to a strong foundation. We all know what we really need—when we stop to ask.

EMILY

Core Work

Emily slides into her car and slams the door shut. She is in her midforties and has blond (with help from the bottle) shoulder-length hair, a face that turns men's heads, and a forward lean into the world that gets her what she wants. She turns the key in the ignition. Her silver Acura, recently detailed, is free of paper scraps or muffin crumbs. Bluetooth turns her car into a giant cell phone, which is synced to her computer, which is synced to her calendar. She dials my number.

"I work with politicians," she tells me. "I help them step forward as leaders, training them to speak from the core of who they are, to access their authentic desire to serve their constituents. I have a great track record. The results are tangible. I love what I do, and I'm real good at it," she says.

She pauses. Something noisy sits in the silence. I wait for her to continue, in her own time. "Even with all I have going for me, something is missing. I feel empty. Here I am, training leaders to step forward from their center when my own core is depleted." Her voice cracks. And then in a brisk, "let's move on" voice, she says, "I guess that's it, we teach what we need to learn."

In addition to being a consultant, Emily is a highly paid public speaker. Her audiences sit up and pay attention. She is refreshingly present, has a snappy wit, and dishes the truth with a smile. Everyone walks away with insight and action steps.

The voice she shares with me in private is sad.

We meet in my office seven days later. She is wearing gray slacks, a red lightweight sweater, and low black heels. Even at five feet four inches tall, she fills the room with her presence. She's sitting still, but I feel her mind calculating, assessing. A gold band on her wedding finger is her only jewelry. Her cell phone, turned off, sits on the pine table in front of her.

"Something feels hollow. Empty," Emily says. "I don't want my to-do list to be at the center of my life, the thing around which everything revolves. I want another kind of center, another kind of container, one that carries me from the inside out, rather than the other way around."

"Tell me more about what you are thinking," I say.

"I have a sense that I'm connected to something larger than me. I know it, I feel it, and then in an instant I lose touch with it. I want to do something that will remind me on a regular basis, something that will be integral to my life. How do I do that?"

"It's not something I can tell you," I answer. "How you do that is very personal to you. I think if you stop and go inside, you'll discover that you already know. Take a moment to get quiet."

After a few moments of quiet, she opens her eyes.

"If I start my days with a routine, not an exercise routine, more like a daily practice, I'm hoping that will remind me deep at my core that I'm connected to something larger than my personal story," she says.

Her eyes soften. A smile emerges. Her face is radiant.
She is sitting tall in her chair, her body quiet. Afternoon
light shimmers on sun-yellow walls. I'm sitting across the
table from Emily. Fifteen years her senior, I am moved
by what she is looking for. Her words could easily be
mine. I stare at the painting on the wall in front of me. A
mountain, rising above a still lake. The painting is very
quiet. The mountain isn't going anywhere. I don't have
any answers for her. Sometimes listening with a big,
open, empathetic heart is what is called for. I practice
stretching my heart. I practice listening to her longing.

"Intellectually I know that we are all one," she says,
"from the same source, many manifestations. What I
know in my head, I don't always know in my heart. I
catch glimpses of it and then, poof, it's gone. That is
what I want this practice to do, to help me know it in my
heart as experience, not intellect."

I ask her to get more specific. "What are the possible
components? How much time would you like to devote
to this practice? Is it daily, five days a week, three days a
week? Twenty minutes, thirty minutes, an hour?"

Emily decides to get up a half hour earlier each
morning to make her new practice part of her life. Not
part of her life, she corrects, the context for her life. It
will serve as her foundation, her core, the place she leads
from as she goes out into the world, the place she retreats
to get recharged.

"I'd like to commit to thirty minutes a day, five days
a week, weekends optional. It will be some combination
of meditation, movement, singing, and reading
inspirational texts. It will be my time to get centered and

go inward. The form is not as important to me as the commitment to show up every day," she says.

In the beginning she sends me an e-mail every day. This keeps her accountable and gives both of us a way to notice what is working and what needs to get tweaked: "I sat today" or "Oops, I missed today." While an important aspect of our work is the accountability, without my support she could send herself daily e-mails to review at the end of the week, or make notes in a journal. That could be part of her practice too.

She arrives at a process that works for her. "I get up in the morning, swing my feet out of bed, plant them on the floor, humor the conversation that goes on in my head, and I keep my body moving until I find my butt on the meditation cushion. Then I sit."

I smile at what she's inventing for herself. "That's right," I say. "To create a practice, begin by showing up. That's step one. Your mind may calm down after a time. It may not. Keep showing up."

We evaluate after two weeks. She tells me that having a set time in the morning really works. She doesn't have to think about it. She knows that at 6:30 she has a date with herself. She also finds that committing to five days a week, weekends optional, makes the rhythm easier. There's consistency. Get up, go to her practice space. Once she gets there, the ingredients can change. Some days, meditation. Some days, readings. Some days, dancing. She trusts her instincts enough to let the content be fluid.

We keep checking in each week. How is the practice going? What's working? What could be tweaked? After several months, the practice becomes automatic. It becomes part of her routine. But more than that, it frames her life. It is the lens through which she sees the world. Most days it reminds her that she is connected with some larger reality. Some days the connection is strong. Some days it is faint and elusive. No matter, she keeps showing up.

"I talked with one of my clients last week," Emily reports late in the process. "He's been avoiding taking action on an important education issue that he really believes in. In the same way my practice brings me to a deeper place in myself, I asked him to stop for a moment, go deep inside, and remember why he ran for office. In that moment he reconnected with his passion, and the knowledge that others are counting on him to step forward as a courageous leader. It wasn't what I said that made the difference, because I've said it before. It was where I was coming from, plugged into something larger than myself, that had him sit up and listen. The next day he made a powerful speech that moved the conversation forward!" she says.

Both of us are beaming. "Your work is serving those who serve. Your clients hire you because they want to make a difference in their political work. Sometimes they forget what brought them to office. Sometimes they get sidetracked or stuck and they need someone who will get them back on course," I tell her. "When you are centered and clear, your work is more powerful, the work of your clients is more effective. There is a ripple effect and everyone wins."

CLARE

The Bind

Overwhelmed, Clare calls me. "Davia, I can't keep up this pace. There is no time for me, and there's not much left of me for everyone else."

She is thirty-eight, has two sons under ten, and a husband over forty. Sometimes she feels as if she has three sons. She loves kids and is completing her master's degree in early childhood education. Clare is even and steady, doesn't raise her voice or snap at her boys, has a long mane of curly hair and a gentle, doe-like quality. She doesn't ever appear to get agitated or anxious. Despite what others see, she knows that her insides are wound tight. Her mind won't stop whirring, and she grinds her teeth at night.

She calls me from her car, in a mall parking lot— the only place calm enough to have this conversation. The call is sandwiched between her last class and going home to fix dinner. Henry is home with the boys. She is parked in the shade of a sycamore, her windows rolled up to mute the noise of late afternoon shoppers. Clare is the maypole around which her family dances. She cooks, cleans, does the bedtime rituals, schedules family events, translates conversations between father and son, son and father. There is no such thing as time or space for Clare.

"What centers you or grounds you?" I ask. "What makes you feel expansive, rather than shut down, what makes you feel as if there is some solid foundation beneath your feet?"

I trust my clients. I draw out what they already know, but don't always realize, and build from there.

"Yoga," she says without hesitating. "But I only go on Sunday mornings. It's a good time for me to go. Henry stays with the boys. It isn't too disruptive— he can manage for the two hours that I'm out of the house. But once a week isn't enough. It only carries me part way through the week and then I begin to tighten up again. I want to go to the Tuesday night class, but then Henry would have to put the boys to bed. He's not really up to it. I can just imagine getting home from a relaxing yoga class to be greeted by three wild boys. That would really make me mad. The kids are used to having me put them to bed. I don't think they'd even let Henry put them to bed. He just wouldn't do it right."

We dig a little deeper. "Tell me what your yoga class provides for you," I say.

"I go into the class, sit on my mat, relax into a pose, and breathe deeply. Being in class is like dipping myself in peacefulness. For an hour and a half, I am reminded who I am at my essence. I remember that I am emotionally strong, that I am generous, and that I have so much to give. I know it deep in my body. From deep within my core I exude spaciousness. I carry it with me after the class and can dip back into the space when the chaos erupts around me. But to really be able to live from that place, I need to be in class more than once a week. There's a yoga pose called a bind. That's where I am, in a bind."

Clare's schoolbooks are in the backseat, a baseball on the floor, one of Henry's wrenches near it. The yoga mat is in the trunk. Her life in miniature. She carries her family wherever she goes. With the windows rolled up against the parking lot noise, the car's interior is getting hot and stuffy.

"Let's talk about putting the kids to bed," I say. "Is there a right way? What is your way? What is Henry's way?" The conversation starts to reveal things that are surprising to Clare. She begins to notice how much she wants things done her way. The bind tightens. This is not the direction she thought the conversation would go.

"Can you see what we have here?" I ask. "We have a neat little puzzle. Here are some of the pieces. Piece number one: You know that yoga is the calming, quieting, element that allows you to be more peaceful and present with your family. You know that you really need to go to class at least two times a week to find the centering you hunger for. Piece number two: You think that your way of putting your children to bed is the right way and that Henry is not capable of putting them to bed correctly. Piece number three: You want to feel you can count on Henry as a father and a husband. You're beginning to notice how much you want to control certain things. Piece number four: You get mad at Henry for not pulling his weight. Piece number five: Catch twenty-two, the bind. If you don't release some control, you will only be able to go to yoga class one day a week. Piece number six: Nothing will change. Everyone will be cranky."

My words bounce off the walls of Clare's car. She stares out the windshield. I have given her a lot to consider. It has been easy to complain about Henry, how he watches too much TV, how he doesn't know how to put the kids to bed, how he acts like a third child. Now Clare is looking at her role in the matter. He may need some support. While he is able and capable, putting the kids to bed is not something Henry is familiar with, and he might need some training and practice, just as Clare would need help with home repairs, Henry's area of expertise.

"Clare, your situation makes me think of embezzlers," I say. "They can never take a vacation because in their absence, their system may be discovered. As long as you hold tight to doing everything your way, you will continue to feel overwhelmed. You need to learn how to invite Henry to partner with you."

We continue to explore.

"What do you want for yourself? What do you want for you and Henry? How can you talk about what you want in a way that he can hear you?" I ask. "You know, this is your area of expertise, raising kids. You've had years of experience, both personally and professionally. It's the place you feel confident. Not so for Henry. His dad was an absent dad. His mother doted on him. He was never expected to participate in running the house, or raising the kids. He doesn't have the social skills that you have. It's all a bit of a mystery to him. This is your opportunity, not only to train Henry, but to train your sons. You can take time for yourself, and you'll bring boys into the world who can see beyond themselves. No small contribution."

Clare sees the pattern clearly, and she very courageously steps up to change it. She and Henry sit down and talk about bedtime rituals. From our conversation she sees that child-rearing is her turf, both as a mother and as a professional, but she is careful not to hold that over Henry. Rather, she engages Henry with graciousness, in partnership. They agree about the importance of bedtime rituals and routines. They decide to experiment. Clare will take Monday, Wednesday, Friday, and Saturday; Henry will take Sunday, Tuesday, and Thursday nights. They also agree about what should be included in the bedtime routine: a wind-down period, a room cleanup, putting on pajamas, brushing teeth, getting settled in bed for story time. Clare likes to read from a book. Henry is a natural storyteller. On his nights, he'll tell stories. On Clare's nights, she'll read stories. They go to the kids together and tell them about the new routine. Everyone will have to rise to the occasion.

"We had a great conversation," Clare says. "It wasn't exactly easy. After so many years of my pushing Henry to the side and not really including him in the process, he wasn't running at me like a happy dog, ready to lick my face. I think he's a little gun-shy. But the good news is that with me at yoga class on Tuesday nights, he can get started with me out of the house, without me standing in judgment from the other room."

Clare starts taking yoga class on Tuesday night. It is

the quiet, reflective, rejuvenating space she needs. The more space she takes for herself, the less she resents Henry. The less she resents Henry, the more she likes him. The boys pick up on the shift.

"Davia, the four of us sat on the couch last night and watched a football game on television together!" she tells me. "You know how much disdain I have for the television. But I'm learning to give a little and not be so rigid about everything. My kids were shocked that I was sitting with them, let alone that it was to watch a football game. I'm embarrassed to admit that it was kind of fun! If I want family time, I guess I can learn to bend and do some of the things that Henry and the kids like to do. After all, yoga is about being flexible."

Clare completed her master's program and was hired to work part time in an early childhood education program. She brings her real-life experience to the mothers, fathers, caregivers, guardians of the children. She's still dizzyingly busy. And she brings her new sense of spaciousness with her wherever she goes.

CYNTHIA

Time and Space

"I'm a writer, but no one really takes me seriously," Cynthia tells me on our first call. "Friends call at anytime and want to chat, and they get annoyed when I say I'm writing. I guess they think because I write at home I can be interrupted at anytime, that what I'm doing isn't real somehow. Maybe there's a way that I don't take myself seriously. I'm constantly being pulled into the rest of the house to do the dishes or talk to the plumber or stare at the weeds in the yard. I need help. I want to reorganize my life so that my writing is a real priority. I know you're a writer and a coach. I assume you understand the challenge and can help me figure out how to create some kind of structure that will keep me focused and keep my pen on the page."

Cynthia is a relatively new writer. After ten years in the corporate world, she threw down her suit and courageously took up the pen. Already her work has been widely published, and she's won several awards for her insightful, quirky fiction. She has intense gray eyes, a long, gray braid, and a sharp tongue. A tiny bedroom at the back of the house, right off the kitchen, serves as her office. The windows are covered with heavy, dark drapes, originals to the old Spanish house, and air circulates slowly in and out of the folds.

There is a small desk, a metal file cabinet, and a desk lamp. Notably absent is a sturdy writing chair. In her file cabinet is a file labeled "rejections," the paper trail chronicling her circuitous journey as an emerging writer. She is proud of the rejections, a testament to her courage, a demonstration of commitment.

"I understand the challenge," I say. "Yes, I am familiar with a writer's life. You and I know that writers dig and excavate and turn things over and over, and whether their work is fiction or nonfiction, they wrestle with the words and the stories those words tell. They push up against hard places, frustrating places, and places devoid of light. Cynthia, your skill and expertise as a writer are already established. What's missing is structure of the right size and shape to move your process forward. A structure that is too constrained will suffocate it, and one that is too porous won't contain your thoughts. One that is just right will encourage and inspire and awaken your creativity. Let's explore what works for you," I say.

Cynthia has been writing at home for years, she tells me. Up at 5:30, she takes her cup of coffee to her office just beyond the kitchen, where she journals for an hour before her boys get up. Alarms go off at 6:30, and the cyclone of activity begins. Pour the breakfast cereal, make the sandwiches, pack the book bags, pull a sweatshirt over her ripped T-shirt and slippers over her bare feet, drive the carpool while hiding behind oversized sunglasses, return home, change to jogging shoes, walk the dog, take a shower. Go back to the room beyond the kitchen. Open the journal, try to pick up where she left off. Pause to make a dentist appointment, go back to writing, pause to pay some bills, go back to writing, get up and go into the kitchen to make a snack, go back to writing, stop to pick up the kids, help with homework, sneak in a few sentences, make dinner, more homework. At the end of the day, she may have a few sentence fragments, or maybe a page or two of good writing, but no real sense of a finished piece coming together. Go to bed and start again the next day.

"It doesn't work," she says. "I put my writing after everything else. I'm mom, wife, friend first. It's not what I want. I see it in everything I do. I'm pissed at my kids, my husband, my dog. But really I'm pissed at me. Something's got to give. I want to rip those heavy drapes right off the wall, but all that would get me is a view of my neighbor's ugly wall. Arrgh. I need to do something more substantial than that," she growls.

"I've been thinking about getting an office, outside of the house. When I had my consulting business, working with corporate clients, I had my own office. It was a place to go, my own special place, which made it easier to separate home life from work life. It made a big difference," she says. "I think it would really support my writing work to be able to leave the house Cynthia is a woman of action. She finds a beautiful space with thick walls, which she paints a soothing tan color. The space is a tangible reminder that her writing is important. There is crown molding at the ceiling and large windows that let in light from the south and the east. Cynthia settles into the space, puts her pens and pencils away, sets up her files. She brings a slouchy couch, two favorite paintings, and her desk from the house, and splurges on a sturdy desk chair. A blue scarf hangs on the wooden coat rack, a pair of hoop earrings sits next to the phone. On the wall above the couch she hangs a large print of five-inch red ankle-strap heels kicking out of the frame. This is Cynthia's space. Soft. Quick witted. Inviting. Contained.

After several weeks in the new office, we discuss during a coaching call how the move is going. "Moving out of the house was definitely a good move, but we're not there yet. I notice I'm still putting other things before my writing. I don't know how to draw the lines. I don't know how to let the phone ring without answering it or leave the e-mail till the end of the day. It's still a challenge to set aside a block of time and sit down to write," she tells me.

"Let's explore what works best for you as a writer," I say. "How long do you like to write? What time of day is best? Do you make an outline, or is the process more organic? What else do you know about how you work?"

She experiments. She comes up with an initial plan. Arrive at her office at 9, after the morning breakfast-carpool-dogwalking rush. Take a half hour to rustle around, make coffee, read e-mail in a cursory way, listen to phone messages. Then for the next three hours, write. Take no calls, read no e-mails, eat no food. Get up and walk around, look out the window, all in the service of writing. Bring lunch. At half past noon, take a forty-five minute break. Go outside. Walk around the neighborhood. Smile at strangers. Make contact. Come back refreshed.

Two afternoons a week teach a writing class. One afternoon attend to personal business, hair, therapist, grocery—all the tasks that used to distract her when she scattered them through her hours and days. Home by 4 o'clock to help with homework and be a mom presence for two teenage boys.

Cynthia experiments with this structure for two weeks. There are the same number of hours in the day, and the same tasks—all of which get done—but now there's a structure. And instead of being constricting, it's liberating. "Davia, I'm a writer!" she says. Her voice is giggly. She is bouncing up and down in her chair. Something has shifted. This is a different woman speaking to me. The office is sparkling, light pouring in from the south.

"Talk to me," I say.

"Here's what works," she replies. "Just knowing that writing time is scheduled makes my life easier. I don't worry that I have to push things aside to make room for it. Instead, I start with the writing and make everything else move over. I feel as though I have more time rather than less. I don't really understand how that happens. Things are easier. I've only been doing this for two weeks, but a rhythm is setting in. It is beginning to feel almost automatic, like my body knows what's next, and I just follow along, ready with my pen and paper."

Other things become easier, clearer. She tells the boys they are in charge of making their own lunches. They grumble a bit but see that she is serious. She puts an auto-reply on her e-mail: "I'm writing. It may take me a few days to get back to you."

It's subtle, but concrete. She carries her identity as a writer in her body. Shoulders back, head up. Her friends come to expect this is her work. Her writing classes fill. Her students bring a new level of commitment with them, a reflection of her commitment to her own writing. Bonus: A new fiction story is published, accompanied by a thoughtful note from the publisher.

At home the impatience dissolves. Unexpectedly, she feels more available for her kids. Knowing that her writing time is now sacred time, she has more attention for her children and her husband. She is not worried they will keep her from her desk.

That is the irony: Structure and discipline create freedom.

TAKEAWAY

Daily practices—whether they are yoga, meditation, better rest, setting aside uninterrupted time—are all building blocks of your personal foundation. The foundation you're laying so carefully is your core, your center, your connection with a larger force. A consistent commitment to a practice allows something important to arise: a sturdy container for something fragile, something intangible. Vision. Purpose. Your most precious offering to the world. They need shelter, support. A sense of spaciousness. A home.

Chapter Two

Take Notice

Papers pile up, closets get too full, apologies go undelivered. One month of no exercise turns into one year. And we're oblivious. We don't notice. Then one day we look up and can't figure out how we gained weight, didn't manage to write that book, and lost touch with a friend.

Often we don't look up because we're afraid of what we might confront. Some part of us goes to sleep, stops seeing. We're averting our eyes from pain, anger, grief, and shame. We turn our heads, close our hearts, and lose a measure of our aliveness. Our world gets smaller and smaller.

Change begins with taking notice. It requires stepping outside of ourselves, standing back and observing with the unemotional curiosity of an archeologist or a detective. Letting go of judgment, commentary, and opinions. Seeing with more objective eyes the person before us, the courageous human, doing and being the best that we know how.

It is not easy. Some days we can't bear to look. Our arrogance, stinginess, and failures flash neon before our eyes. We are not the people we want to be.

Noticing takes practice. There is power in noticing without judging. Something lightens, something loosens, and something gets freed up.

MY LESSON

Five-Minute Rule

When someone asks, I say yes. Whether it's for a favor, an opinion, or a date. I want to be helpful, I want to be a good guy, I want people to like me. So I say yes, even when it makes no sense. Even when it gets me into trouble.

A friend invited me to a play. I said yes and wrote it in my calendar. A few days later, another friend invited me to an all-day event on the same day as the play. I said yes. And we could go to dinner after the event, she continued. "Great," I said. I actually watched myself open my mouth and say yes, knowing I'd committed to being at the play. I knowingly put myself in a bind. Then I really had a problem. Telling the truth didn't seem like a good option. Lying didn't seem like a good option. I wiggled out of the play by telling a story that was midway between truth and lie. It felt awful.

A week later a neighbor called and asked whether I would watch his two-year-old son for two hours on a Thursday afternoon. "Sure," I said, jumping at the opportunity to be helpful. I work at home and make my own hours, and sometimes I forget that I'm at work. I watched myself say yes, knowing that I had work to do. As soon as I hung up the phone, I started railing at myself. "You're supposed to be writing! Why are you putting his needs before yours?" I asked myself in a less than gracious voice. I gave myself five minutes, calmed down, and called him back and told him I was sorry I couldn't watch his son after all because I needed to work, but please ask again.

Every time this happened I put myself through the ringer, cursed under my breath, called myself unpleasant names, and swore up and down that it would never happen again. Slowly I began to simply take notice, without so much judgment, that this was simply what I did: I always said yes.

I started to pay more attention. Why did I keep doing this? I wanted to be liked. I wanted to matter. I didn't want to disappoint. I thought saying yes would get me what I wanted. But it didn't. One friend was mad, the other disappointed.

My sister has a five-minute rule. When I ask her something she usually says no, and then adds, ask me again in five minutes, I'll probably change my mind. I need a five-minute rule. When someone asks now, I say, "Let me check. I'll get back to you in five minutes." That gives me the time I need to answer in a way that supports me.

MONICA

Cat in the Sun

"I'm so ready to start this coaching work with you," Monica says.

This is our first conversation, and like most of my work, it's over the phone. I want to "see" her office and get a sense of what it feels like to be sitting at her desk. "Paint me a picture. Describe where you are so I can see you in your space," I say.

"My office is piled with unfiled papers," she tells me. "From my desk chair, I can see into the kitchen, where dirty dishes are stacked on the counter. There's a long, low side table next to my desk that's covered with my kids' stuff—math problems, handwriting practice sheets, a piano lesson book. I'd say I'm sitting in a low level of chaos."

I'm interested in her description of the space, and the mess. But on the phone I'm also able to listen without being distracted by visual information, which tends to overpower the other senses. I hear, with my whole being, the words, the tone and inflection of voice, breathing, where she pauses, and when her sentences run on gasping for air. I explain this to Monica, and tell her that as we work together, she will strengthen your own noticing muscle.

A rubber dog bone is buried behind her office door

and her cat is curled on the carpet in the sun, she tells me. An overstuffed chair sits in front of long southwest-facing windows. The clock ticks on the wall. A large dry-erase calendar is tacked to her wall, a red marker on the floor under her desk. Snow blankets the yard. "It's a mess. It looks like a baby hurricane hit," Monica says. "There are papers all over the desk. Most of them are mine, but some belong to the kids. My office seems to have a magnetic force. Everyone gets drawn in here: the kids, the cat, the dogs."

Monica is a successful public health consultant with clients all over the state. She gets up early, before her kids, before her husband, before the dogs and cat, does her public health work, pauses to wake up the kids, make breakfast, pack lunches, and drive the carpool, then returns to a quiet house. She schedules her work meetings between 9 and 2. Girl Scouts, piano, soccer, and the dentist after 3.

"I'm listening for what you notice about your surroundings, but I also listen for what you have stopped noticing. Everything gives me information. I'm curious about how you construct your world, what your assumptions are, how you live based on those assumptions. There are clues everywhere. My job is to notice them and to train you to notice them. There is freedom in seeing things as they are," I say.

A bird is singing outside my window. A blue bowl with three gray stones sits on my desk. Sun fills the room. My own cat is curled by the heater vent.

"Get up from your desk," I say. "Find a place to sit where you can't see the dirty dishes, and you can't see the unfiled papers on your desk, and you can't see the kids' homework on the side table. Find a quiet place that feels calming, that doesn't distract you, a place that lets you breathe and relax."

She sits in the overstuffed chair. The chair is warmed by the sun. Her mother's tatting covers the armrests. Her feet rest on a needlepoint footstool, next to her cat. She has to-do lists and half-finished projects in every room of the house. Everyone in her life makes requests; her church, the kids' school, clients, her kids, her husband. Notably, her own name is not on the list.

"This feels good," she says. "Just moving from my desk gives me a little space to think and breathe. I feel like I get blown by the wind wherever it wants to take me, and nothing ever gets grounded or takes root."

We sit with those words for a moment. "The first step in noticing is to create some distance," I tell her. "That literally gives you a new perspective. By walking away from the whirlwind of your office and sitting in another chair, you take yourself out of the picture. From the new vantage place you can observe with a little detachment. When things get too confusing or frustrating, take a few deep breaths, get up and go stand someplace else! Here is what I noticed as you were speaking. You used the word *wind* a few times," I add. "You said your desk looks like it was hit by a baby hurricane, and you feel like you get blown by the wind and nothing takes root. When you moved to the overstuffed chair, a sturdy, solid chair, you started to feel grounded and were able to think more clearly. I listen for what you want and need, and you tell me in a variety of ways, ways that you are not even aware of. Right now, you are telling me you want to balance the wind with stillness and rootedness. Now we get to discover what form and shape that takes."

Sitting in the chair with the cat curled at her feet, she finds quiet. In her professional work, she promotes health, well being, and balance. She is beginning to notice the imbalance in her own life. Too much wind, not enough earth. Perpetual motion, absence of stillness.

Nothing seems quite as urgent from the sturdy chair. She takes a deep breath.

There is silence on the phone. She takes herself out of her own whirlwind and enters a new space. "I know what it is. I know what I need." She is excited. "I need cat-in-the-sun time." We both know exactly what she means.

She decides to begin to pay attention and listen to her body—to slow down, pause, take cat-in-the-sun-time. When she feels stuck with a project, or has to make a challenging call, she will get up and move to her chair, takes cat-in-the-sun-time until she feels revitalized and re-inspired.

"From where I'm sitting it's obvious that I need to clear my desk. It's hard to be creative with so much competing for my attention. I'd like to commit to spending a few hours once a week to sorting through papers, filing or tossing, until the surface of my desk is clear," Monica says.

"Let me ask you a question. What do you know about how you get things done? Do you work well by doing a task once a week for several hours at a time?

Does breaking it down to daily increments of fifteen to twenty minutes work well for you? What time of day works best? Do you like to do the hard things first and the easy things last or the other way around? Great that you want to clear your desk. Keep in mind that you want it to stay clear. What system can you put in place that will support that? Use this week as an experiment and notice what works best for you," I say.

"Good call!" she says. "I think you've hit on something. Now that I think about it, I'm not sure that trying to clear for several hours at a time will really happen. Something will always be more important. But maybe if I do a little every day in the morning when I feel fresh, I might have a chance of keeping a clear desk. Like you said, I'll use this week to experiment."

Each week I send my clients a form to fill out and send back to me before our call. It is the summary of their week. I ask what worked, what didn't work, what they got done, what they didn't, what they noticed. It is useful for both of us. It gives my clients a chance to stop and reflect. It's so easy to move on and not even notice the strides we are taking, the muscles that are incrementally getting stronger. This shines a light on their work. It gives me more information to use in our coaching work.

I read Monica's form before our next call. There are exclamation points all over the page.

"I decided that initially I would spend three hours this week filing and tossing just to get the desk to a manageable place!!! I did that the very first day and oh, it was so satisfying!!! Now I'm spending fifteen minutes every morning clearing and filing and making a plan for the day. One thing I discovered is that my eyes are always bigger than my stomach. In this case, I always think I can do more in a day than I actually have hours for. So I'm cutting back and committing to fewer things in a day!!! What a concept! Maybe, just maybe, I can't do it all. And maybe, just maybe, it's not my job to do it all! It's been an amazing week."

When she is offered a contract that involves lots of driving and evening meetings, before doing anything, she goes to sit in her chair for cat-in-the-sun time. From this place, it becomes clear that the evening meetings interfere with family time. She turns down the contract, confident that something more appropriate will take its place. The whirlwind that defined her life at the beginning of our work is shifting. She is taking time to pause, interrupting her constant motion with stillness.

"Oh, I feel like I have so much more time. Everything seems easier. I thought it was because I don't have as much work and then I realized that no, that's not true, I actually have more work! My office desk is clear, my thinking is clear, that howling wind is now a gentle breeze."

ROBIN

Learning to Ask

"I don't know how to make this relationship work," Robin says. "Whenever I get within six feet of my girlfriend, my brain shuts down."

We're sitting in my home office, a high-ceilinged room on the second floor of a 1920s Spanish courtyard building. Light is pouring in the high windows, reflecting off the butter yellow walls. Robin's chair is pushed in close to the long, pine table. His thumb and index finger are running back and forth across his chin. He is in his midforties and has a deep furrow between his eyebrows, a hint of gray at his temples, and a one-day beard.

"You know a lot about yourself, but you don't always have access to that knowledge," I tell him. "My job is to give you access to the wisdom you already have. You get to that wisdom by discovering where you are right now, by standing at a distance and observing yourself. Think of yourself as an archeologist or a detective in your own life."

Robin stares down at the knots in the pine table. With his right hand capped over his left, he squeezes his knuckles together. I sit across from him, quietly enjoying the way the table is wide enough to give emotional and physical space, solid enough to lean on. My pen sits uncapped next to a writing pad. As he squeezes his hands together, his forearms flex, revealing strong and clearly defined muscles. I suspect he will find the same strength in his character that I see in his body.

"Begin by noticing," I tell him. "Let's discover what you know about your relationship with your girlfriend. Fear shuts down our ability to think clearly. I bet there are things you are thinking about your relationship that you don't feel safe admitting to yourself, let alone saying out loud. This is the place to practice saying the scary, dark thoughts out loud. Once they're out on the table you can stand back and look them over. They may just lose some of their scariness. Tell me what else you notice when you want to talk with your girlfriend," I say.

"I open my mouth to speak and I stutter and mumble and repeat things. I forget what I want. My words add up to nothing. It's just a garble of nonsense. Then, worse than forgetting and sounding like an idiot, I end up agreeing to things I don't even want. I get so mad at myself. I feel like a big liar. Why can't I just say what I want? Why is that so hard?" he says.

"Practice telling me what you want," I say.

He looks up from the table. "I want time to be alone. Lisa always wants to be with me, day and night. I really need time for me when I'm not joined at the hip with someone else. I like to read and hike alone. I remember who I am when I'm alone. Sometimes I just like to sit and stare, but that's never a possibility with Lisa. I don't know how to tell her what I want. I feel selfish, like I don't love her as much as she loves me. And that makes me a bad boyfriend. I should want to be with her as much as she wants to be with me. So now I resent her, because she doesn't give me what I want, and she makes me feel like I'm doing something wrong."

I nod. "Thank you. That is very clear to me. Here's what I heard you say: You want time to be alone. Being alone reminds you who you are. You think it's selfish to want alone time, and if you loved Lisa as much as she loves you, you wouldn't want time alone. You don't know how to tell her what you want, and yet you're mad at her for not giving you what you want," I say.

"Hmm. Just hearing it repeated back to me gives me a slightly different perspective. I don't think I ever really heard myself say that thing about Lisa loving me more 'cause she wants to be with me all the time. Maybe it's not about love, maybe some of the time she's afraid to be alone. That's a radical thought! Maybe she doesn't love me more, just differently," Robin smiles.

"You have different needs. Can you see that?" I ask. "You want some alone time. Lisa wants more together time. Consider that as a piece of information. Not good or bad, not more loving or less loving, just a preference. Tell me how that sounds to you."

Robin is staring down at the table, flicking his thumb and index finger. The furrow in his forehead is softening.

"Maybe. I still can't imagine telling her. The irony is that she wants time with me, but I'm so mad because I'm not getting alone time that when we spend time together, I'm not even really there. I'm sort of caved in on myself. I'm sure I'm no fun to be with. If I actually took the time I needed to be alone, then I would probably be much more fun to be with when we are together. Now there's a wild thought. I didn't know any of this until we started having this conversation. Is this what you mean by noticing?" he says.

"Exactly," I say. "Now, before you go back to Lisa, tell me what you want. Don't think about Lisa. Just talk to me. Be really specific. You can even write some notes in your book."

"I want one or two nights a week to go out to the studio and paint or read or write. No interruptions. I want it to be the same night every week so it's a given, that's what I'm doing and I don't have to think about it or negotiate for it every week," he says.

He's beaming. His voice is deep and resonant and his words are absolutely clear. This is not the same person who came to me tongue-tied and frustrated.

"Write it down," I say. "Go back to Lisa. Your job is to watch yourself in your interaction with her. Notice. Yes, you're aiming to tell her you want two nights a week. That may or may not happen. Your main job is to notice the course of the conversation. It will give us more information."

He goes to Lisa. This time he wears his get-curious cap, gathering data about his behavior as well as hers. They have a conversation. He makes a big discovery.

"Wow!" he says to me, "I never even asked for what I wanted! I got scared and my mind went a little wacky. I never even said, 'I want to be alone Tuesday and Thursday nights.' I can't believe it. That may have something to do with why she doesn't give me what I want. I don't ask!"

A very valuable piece of information.

"I think I ask for what I want. But I don't. I'm vague. I allude. I intimate. I'm not direct. I skirt around. And then I'm surprised and annoyed when I don't get what I want," he says. "And I can see now, Lisa is not the only one I do this with."

Robin traces a thread that he now sees runs throughout the tapestry of his life. He's vague, unclear, and indefinite with people at work, with his friends, with his kids, with his family, with the cable guy, with the waiter. Vague, unclear, and indefinite with everyone.

Because he has taken this step outside himself, he isn't immediately harsh or self-critical. He is standing back and noticing. He notices how it damages his relationships, how it keeps him from having what he wants, how it keeps him perpetually annoyed.

It has been easier to point a finger at his girlfriend and blame her for his tangle than to open his mouth and ask for what he wants. It has been easier to complain about all the people who don't listen and don't give him what he wants than to step forward. But now he is ready. He's tired of feeling defeated.

We start slowly with two goals: make clear requests, and do what he says he will do. These are huge goals, and require practice. He starts making small requests and practices saying yes to the things he really intends to do. Each week his speaking and follow-through muscles get stronger, and better defined.

He tells his sons he'll call on Tuesday. He does. He pays his overdue phone bill. He stops Lisa in the middle of a tricky conversation and says he's not ready to have this conversation right now. He isn't apologetic, simply straightforward. She listens.

More of Robin starts to surface. He is flexing muscles, inside and out.

He still doesn't feel ready to ask for his alone time. But he can see that he is moving in the right direction. Each action, each conversation is a building block in support of bigger and trickier conversations.

ANNA

The Manager Inside

Anna calls me from her office, excited and slightly panicked. "I've just been promoted from my staff position to a management position. Starting tomorrow I'm going to be managing the very people who today are my peers. Yikes! Can you make me into a manager?" she says.

Her employer, a successful nonprofit that promotes education for girls in developing countries, fills the entire eleventh floor of an old, stone building. Anna has been on staff there three years. She has never been a manager. Her small cubby has a desk, a metal file cabinet, three bookshelves, and a floor-to-ceiling window. A large calendar is tacked to the soft walls of her movable office. The leaves on the maple trees bordering the street below are turning reds and yellows. On her desk is a goofy, smiley photo taken at the beach, her hair flying, her arm around her honey, a reminder to bring her whimsy into the office. Even over the phone, I can feel Anna's smile. She is generous, kind, and funny.

"Make me into a manager," she repeats. "Wave your magic wand and turn me into a manager." As though Superman's suit gave him the power to fly. As though I could dip her in manager water and she'd come out a manager.

"There is no manager mold," I say. "Managing, leading, collaborating, bringing out the best in others, inspiring others to rise to the occasion—that all comes from the inside out. Every manager has her own signature. You are about to discover yours. I'm not going to turn you into someone else. You are going to become more of who you already are. To do that, you need to begin to notice, find out where you are, what you already know, and where you get stuck."

"OK, I'm game," she says.

"Let's discover what your picture of a manager is. Break it apart and find out what it's composed of. How does she behave? What does she wear? What does she say, and how does she say it? How does she hold her body? Tell me everything you notice about your picture of a manager."

I settle in to listen. Above my desk is a newspaper clipping with a photo of a hawk perched on the ledge of a skyscraper in New York City. Beneath the photo I've tacked a poem, reminding me about heights and fear and courage. In Anna's mind, there is a gap between who she is and the manager she wants to be. She thinks she needs to be someone else or some other way, that who she is, is not sufficient. I understand where Anna is. Years ago I worked for a nonprofit whose larger-than-life mission was to end world hunger. One of my jobs was to ask ordinary, everyday people for large sums of money to fund our work. The first time I got up on a stage in front of a large, crowded room my stomach was lurching and my hands were clammy. Who did I think I was? What gave me permission to make this request? Someone with the right credentials should be up here on this stage, I thought to myself. Someone more knowledgeable, someone who really knows about world hunger, someone who can move people to take bold action.

Anna is quiet. "Oh, I don't know," she finally says. "A manager is very efficient, doesn't kid around, always has a serious, no-nonsense attitude. She wears a tight skirt with a matching jacket, her hair is short and efficient, her lipstick's red. She never seems to relax, is always in motion, and has a bit of a bite when she talks to her staff," Anna says. "And that's not me, I'm not like that, and I don't want to be anything like that. Eww."

We both laugh. The specter of the mythic manager begins to dissipate, losing some of its power.

"Do you know anyone who fits that description?" I ask.

"Well, I know people who have some of those qualities, but certainly not all of them. My boss isn't anything like that. He's very relaxed and available. He's not judgmental, and he's a great listener. And he definitely doesn't wear a tight skirt or red lipstick!" She laughs.

I'm looking at the photo of the hawk on the ledge, holding my pen in my left hand. The poem beneath the photo is about coming to the edge of all that you know, then stepping off and learning to fly. It makes me think of Anna.

"Take a look at yourself. What do you notice? What qualities do you value about yourself? What is it you love about yourself—as a human being?" I ask.

"I'm a great listener. I'm easygoing, and I have a

quick wit. I love to collaborate with a team, and people really trust me. When I try to be that other manager, my brain freezes. I can't think clearly, and I end up saying stupid things. I'm so busy trying to be someone I'm not that I end up tripping all over myself. I get all serious, and I'm no fun to be around. And frankly, my sense of humor is one of the best things I've got going for me. It relaxes people, then there's an intimacy that gets created which makes for great collaboration," Anna admits.

"Don't lose any of those qualities," I say to her. "That is why you, Anna, were promoted. Don't turn into someone else. Manager is not some costume you step into. It's the other way around. The more you, Anna, step forward, the more the manager Anna will emerge. This week, go back to your job and notice when you are trying to be the tight-skirted, red-lipstick manager and when you are letting Anna, the generous quick wit, run the show. Come back with stories."

On our next call, she's bubbling over. "Davia, we had a managers meeting the other day," she says. "Eight of us around an oval table in the conference room, with our computers and iPhones and writing tablets. I was nervous at first and noticed that I wanted to just kind of slip behind the tight-skirted, red-lipstick facade. But I didn't. Instead, I took a breath and looked around the room. The meeting started, and right away I had a question. Ugh. At first I kept my mouth zipped, because it seemed like a dumb question, then I realized that if I had the question, maybe others did too, and that I would be doing everyone else a favor by asking it.

So I asked, like it was just me, regular ol' Anna wanting to know something.

"I saw some heads bob up and down. Yep, they were wondering the same thing. It felt good. I even let loose with a few good comebacks. That larger-than-life, mythic manager is not quite as big as she started out to be. If she were a blow-up doll, I'd have to say she's losing some of her air—her hot air, that is! Instead of red lipstick, I showed up, the real Anna. What a relief. Not only that, I noticed that the other managers seemed to lighten up a bit too."

I look at the newspaper clipping above my desk. The hawk seems to be enjoying himself up there on the ledge. Noticing the traffic jam in the street below.

TAKEAWAY

Begin to take notice. Look at things as they are, stripped of opinions, judgments, and commentary.

It's a slow process. We are often blind to our habits. In noticing, we are attempting to step outside of routine patterns and see ourselves from another vantage point—a generous and compassionate place.

One way to begin noticing is to pause when something upsets you. Count to ten. Take a deep breath. Ask yourself with a sense of curiosity what upset you. The initial answer may camouflage an underlying reason. Sometimes it requires some digging. You are mad at a friend because she "holds you hostage" on the phone. On further examination, you discover you are upset because you want to hang up, but don't know how to say goodbye. That's the beginning of the thread. Keep pulling on it to see what gets revealed. You might discover that a straightforward telephone goodbye builds the muscle to ask for a raise.

Step back from yourself and reflect. Do it through journaling, taking quiet time, observing yourself as you walk through your day. What upsets you, what stops you? Where do you get stuck? Where do you get scared? Practice saying, "Hmm, that's interesting," when you observe your own behavior. For the moment, put aside words like good and bad. Just notice.

Notice your relationship with your partner, or children, your attitude toward your work, your relationship toward money, toward your bathroom mirror. There is not a right or wrong place to begin, so start where you are.

There is power in seeing things as they are, without the story we layer on top.

Chapter Three

Clear the Way

Like Goldilocks, we want to make ourselves just right. We want to fit in. We want to be liked. We want to belong. We want to be good enough. We pretend not to be scared. We pretend to know the answers. We deny the parts of us that we don't like, cover up the bits that remind us of our shortcomings. Evidence of our failings gets stuffed into the deepest corners of the closet.

Trouble is, those things don't disappear. They lurk around the edges of our lives, waiting to jump out at any moment. It takes effort to keep them tucked away. It takes energy. It gets tiring, carrying around all those hidden parts of ourselves that we don't want to look at.

There's relief in clearing stuff out, emotional and physical. Knock on your own door, gently, with kindness. Start with whatever is right in front of you. Pull everything out from the dark corners. Hold each thing up to the light. Name it. Own what is yours.

Start to reawaken all the pieces of you that you exiled far beneath the earth's surface. The smelly, the moldy, the irritating parts. Peel away the things that aren't yours, that you no longer need, and let them go. Invite yourself back, one piece at a time.

House as a Metaphor

Within a nine-month period, my daughters left for college and my husband left our marriage. I was lonely, broken, sad, and angry. My house was empty and my life unrecognizable. I missed my husband, I missed my children, I missed my family. I was confused and disoriented. I was without my moorings.

In shock, I moved myself out of our bedroom and slept on a cotton mat in the room down the hall. It felt safer close to the floor. With my knees pulled to my chest, and my thumb pressed to my closed lips, I cried myself to sleep for many weeks.

As I started to regain some sense of self, I made my way back to our bedroom. But before moving back in, I had to clear it, clean it, change it, by literally and figuratively changing the perspective. First, I tackled the bed. I hoisted the mattress, then the box springs, and leaned them up against the wall. Then dismantled the metal headboard and footboard and carted them to the garage, walking sideways down the hall to avoid scratching the walls. The physical exertion was cleansing. The frameless bed found a new home on the east wall and sat solidly on the carpeted floor. I dragged in a chair from the living room for sitting and reading. Then I changed out the faded curtains for floor-length heavy cotton, giving me more privacy. The room began to feel like mine—safe, cozy, and contained.

The house was my living metaphor. By taking apart, rearranging, throwing out, giving away, letting go, I was shaping myself into a new person. I was discovering a new me. The process was chaotic and disorienting.

First, I made repairs: Planing doors that didn't close all the way. Replacing broken window panes. Tightening loose doorknobs. Oiling drawers that didn't slide. Building shelves in closets.

Then I painted. Everything. The house was like a construction site, with all the furniture pushed away from the walls and covered with drop cloths. All the cupboards emptied and the closets cleared out. The walls were cleaned, spackled, and sanded, leaving a fine layer of dust everywhere. At the same time, I took myself down to the studs. I came face to face with my empty, broken, and scared feelings, and knew that those could not be so simply painted over.

Transformation can be a messy business.

But I made a choice. I tore down some walls and opened myself to a new life rather than remain angry and tethered to a past life. Step by step, I rebuilt myself from the inside out.

LESLIE

Inner Space, Outer Space

Eight women sit around a long oak oval table. Wool hats and knitted scarves hang over the backs of their chairs. Today they are strangers. At the end of eight weeks they will cry and laugh and applaud one another. The winter sun is soft and forgiving on the table.

"Welcome," I say. "This workshop is called Inner Space, Outer Space. Each week you will set tasks for yourself. You'll clear your closets, clean your cars, pay off old debts, toss unwanted papers. And in the process you'll discover some invisible link between your outer world and your inner world. When you clear the unwanted, the unused, the broken, and the battered, things lighten up. Life begins to look and feel less weighty. This class is about spaciousness and aliveness."

Leslie introduces herself in her gruff voice. "I don't really know why I came to this class," she says. "Something in the flyer caught my attention." Her jaw is tight, her thick dark braid caught between her scarf and shoulder bag. She sits at the table, fiddling with a stack of papers. Her hands are worn. A large amber ring is loose on her middle finger.

Leslie lives alone in a three-story Victorian. She's been in the house for thirty years, the last fifteen alone. She raised her three sons there. When her grandchildren visit, they sleep in one of the third-floor bedrooms. They play dress-up with all the vintage clothes and beat on the drums. Every room is filled with torn boxes, moldy books, broken musical instruments, paints, metal scraps, odds and ends for possible art projects. Her house gets smaller and smaller. Her world gets smaller and smaller. It's a kind of hardening of the arteries; the pathways that lead her back to her actual creativity are clogged with unnecessary detritus.

"I'm an artist—a ceramicist and a painter. But I'm not doing either. There's no room in my house. It's like I've lost interest, and I don't seem to have enough time. What do I dream of? I have no idea. There's too much in the way to even know. I just don't know. I have no idea. I've kind of given up."

But she joins us anyway. Each week she sets a task for herself. One week she clears her stairs, another week she sifts through a closet. The motor from the dishwasher sits by the door, an annoyance she puts off having fixed. She drags herself to class, moans about how hard it is to give anything away, and then inevitably surprises us with a story about some miracle that arose from the clearing.

"I cleared one room, and then I realized that I could rent it out. I don't know why that never occurred to me before. There's a college right at the end of my street. Kids are always needing a place to live. I could use the company. Not to mention the extra cash. I called the school, and they found me Greg. He's studying architecture and apparently has a talent for fixing things around the house. He moves in next week."

Leslie's braid is held together with a red rubber band. On her notepad is a sketch of three women across the table from her. Her pencil sits on the pad. There is a hint of a smile on her wrinkled face.

"Sounds like things are beginning to open up a bit," I say.

After a few more weeks of sifting and sorting, she comes to class excited. "Greg fixed my dishwasher, I gave my sons a deadline for getting their stuff from the basement, and I used the rent money to pay off an old credit card. But the best part is this—I want to clear out one room in my house and use it as my painting studio." And then very quietly, she adds, "I'd like to have a show of my work."

Around the long oval oak table, the other women are smiling. Leslie has come a long way. She's letting go of a past. She is making room for a present. And a future. Her courage inspires others to make room for their own journey.

"Bravo!" says Henrietta. "Bravo!"

Leslie chooses the room at the top of the stairs for her studio. The best light. The right size. It was her painting studio some years ago. The easel was there. Her paints. Along with boxes of old clothes, unfinished paintings, torn sneakers. She clears and cleans.

"You won't believe this," she says in class the next week. "I just got a letter in the mail from my church. They are having an art show, inviting members of the congregation to show their work. They asked me if I would show my paintings. They want eight pieces—the show is in five weeks. As I was clearing out my studio,

I found five pieces that are already done. I need to do three brand new pieces. I'm so excited."

Eight women around the oval table grin. They are proud. The show gives Leslie a focus. It gives purpose to the clearing. This is the evidence she needs that the clearing is working. The artist is reemerging.

The whole class goes to the show. Eight women gather around the large, vibrant paintings. When they look at the paintings, they see weeks of clearing. They see calls to estranged sons, debts repaid, dishwashers repaired. They see the stories that made it possible for the pictures to be painted, to be hung, to be seen. Eight women see themselves, their own stories, their lives.

ELIZABETH

A Narrow Pathway

"Davia, I'm buried under paper. I can't think anymore. I can hardly make my way to my desk, there are so many papers stacked everywhere—most of which I haven't even looked at for years," Elizabeth says.

Her office has one large window, which looks out on the stone building twenty feet away. There is a narrow path from her office door to her desk. It is flanked by knee-high stacks of papers. There is no visible surface on her desk, and her computer is sandwiched between more stacks of paper. I wonder how she can have a clear thought. Her world is closing in, sucking out the breathing space, the thinking space, the creative space. I see what she has accomplished in spite of this crowding, and I wonder what will be possible when she clears some space for herself.

She is the policy director of a small nonprofit with a big mission, stewarding outdoor space. She is on a first-name basis with many members of Congress. Her primary focus these days, passing legislation to preserve open space, is a huge challenge in the face of political infighting and apathy. In her capacity, she courageously speaks out, often to unreceptive audiences. Yet she persists.

"It's taken you years to collect all these papers," I say when we meet in her office on a Saturday, the only quiet time in the building. "This will take time. Be patient with yourself. Clearing papers may feel small and mundane, but think of it like this: It is that attention to detail, to hundreds of individual conversations with members of Congress, to thousands of conversations with citizens, that makes the difference in the larger conversation. We'll give that kind of attention to this project. Everything is the same as everything else.

"We'll break it down so that it is manageable, so it doesn't seem so daunting. Start by taking a small stack of papers from your office and bring them into the hall. Look at each paper and make three piles: Toss it, keep it, and "not sure." This is the first pass. Go through the papers quickly, and if you hesitate at a piece, put it in the "not sure" pile. We'll look at it later," I say. "Right now we want to get rid of as much as possible, then we can see where we are."

I am sitting on the floor, leaning against the wall. Elizabeth is sitting cross-legged next to the recycling bin. The office is quiet. The overhead fluorescent is our only light. Several paper clips are scattered on the floor.

"I'm excited to begin," Elizabeth says.

It becomes a meditation. I sit with her as she reads and sorts. The choice is hers. I watch. I smile. I encourage. If she hesitates for a second, the paper goes into the "not sure" pile.

"Oh, god," she says, picking up a folder. "These are résumés from two years ago from people who applied for a legislative intern position. I never called them back or even wrote them a note. Ick, that's embarrassing, that's just not right. I kept the résumés thinking someday I would get back to them. Instead, every time I saw them it made me feel small and irresponsible."

I stop her. "Put them aside. Let's not talk about them right now. After we go through everything we'll have a chance to go back, and you can make choices about what you want to do. This clearing process is about completing things so that you're not dragging anything around with you anymore. Don't worry," I say, "we won't sweep anything under the carpet."

Hours pass. Six heavy-duty, black trash bags are lined against the wall. It has grown dark outside. Elizabeth is humming to herself. One whole corner of her office is paper-free.

"Enough for one day," she says.

"I think you are beginning to feel and sense how heavy this weight has been, how you've been buried underneath your papers, and the things that you said you would do that didn't get done," I tell her. "I think you can see how it's slowed you down and clouded your vision."

We come back the next day. I see a change in Elizabeth's face and in her body. Her eyes are brighter. Her shoulders relax. It's exhausting work, but she's energized by it.

"Elizabeth," I say, "you are a champion for a healthy, sustainable planet, a champion for aliveness. Your own aliveness was buried beneath your piles. It was submerged under the weight of people you neglected, unfinished projects, unreturned calls, unwritten notes, unspoken brave new ideas. It shows up in your body, in the pockets of your unconscious. That's true for all of us. It makes us sleepy. Cranky. Heavy. It makes us snap at other people. As you clear the way, everything about you begins to lighten. You can feel it in your body, your shoulders straighten, your eyes sparkle, your breathing deepens. You smile more."

I tell her she is very brave. She picks up piece after piece of paper, looks at all she has pushed aside, assuming that if she ignored it, it would go away. Instead her world became a tiny path with a window staring at a stone wall.

Over the next several weeks, she continues to clean up, and not just the piles of paper. She returns phone calls, writes overdue notes, and finishes projects. Her staff notices. They begin to clean up their offices.

The next year her department is awarded a multimillion-dollar grant from a prestigious foundation. Who knows if there is a causal relationship? All she knows is that they've never gotten a grant anywhere near this size. Elizabeth cleared the way—in all realms. She is celebrating aliveness from the bare corners of her desk, to the cleared communications, to the brave new voice that asked boldly for help. She cleared the space for an astronomical amount of money to support the work that she so values.

BEN

Out of the Basement

"Help! I can't seem to get anything done. I need an office makeover. This doesn't work for me at all. I'm not really sure what to do," Ben says.

Ben works at home. He is a marketing consultant. Clients don't come to him, he goes to them. His basement office is a large, low-ceilinged carpeted space that doubles as a playroom for his two daughters and a storage area for everything that won't fit upstairs. The light comes from dim fluorescents in the ceiling. In his loosely defined work area are two desks, a defunct computer, an outdated copy machine, and a tangle of unused electronic cords. A large dry-erase calendar is tacked on the wall. Two green Lego pieces are on the floor under his desk.

"Let's sit outside your 'office space' and have a conversation," I say after he's given me a tour. "I want you to tell me stories. Tell me about this room; tell me about your office area."

We sit in beanbag chairs, facing the "office space." It feels dark to me. It's not only the lack of light; it feels as though something heavy is sitting in Ben's corner of the room. I wonder what it is. When I first met Ben upstairs, outside in the light, he was bouncy and had a wide grin. Here in the basement his face is long.

"Well," he starts slowly, "all that office furniture is, um, from when I had an outside office and a business partner. We weren't a good match, to say the least. We haven't spoken in over a year, and somehow I ended up with the furniture. I don't use it. I use that little kid desk," he says pointing to the desk in the corner. "I keep intending to do something with the old furniture, but I just haven't managed to. It was expensive," Ben says.

We both take a deep breath. I'm not at all surprised.

"Tell me more," I say, finding another Lego under my beanbag seat. "What happened? Why aren't you and your partner speaking?"

"Lots of things. But I guess it's partly that he's single and works long, long hours. In fact, that's all he does is work. My family is central to my life, and I just didn't want to work in the same way that he did. I think he was jealous. We just couldn't work it out. We divided the clients and I don't know why, but I ended up with the furniture. The weird thing is, I don't even notice the desk, the computer, or the copy machine anymore. Which is pretty funny because they take up a good portion of the room! All I know is that I never want to come down to the basement. I never really thought about why. I take my papers upstairs and clutter up the dining room table. My wife gets annoyed and tells me to go downstairs into my office," he says.

Rows of canned tomatoes sit on the metal shelves in the storage area. A support beam creates a small divide between the play area and the office area.

"Can you see why telling this story is the first step

you need to take before we make your office space work for you? You are lugging around this thing from your past that didn't turn out the way you wanted. But you haven't let it go. Everything you do is built on top of that desk, the defunct computer, and the well of disappointment. Are you ready to end that chapter and move on?"

We are like two children, sitting in our beanbag chairs watching a movie, the movie of the failed business. Ben is twisting his ring on his finger. The fluorescent lights are making a low humming sound. A pink Barbie high heel is on the floor in the play area.

"Wow, just by telling the story of the business I started to see a whole bunch of things. I never really noticed how much Jeff wanted a family," Ben says. "I think several of our disagreements came from his jealousy. Plus there's my own disappointment. This was my first business with a partner. I really wanted it to work. It didn't. And I've never admitted to myself how much I've felt like a failure. And that stupid furniture keeps reminding me that I blew it. No wonder I never want to come down here! OK, I'm ready to let the furniture go."

"How can you make it a win/win? Is there a secondhand store, a family member, a friend who would be delighted to take it off your hands?" I ask.

Ben agrees that by our next meeting he will clear out all things that remind him of his previous business. He wants to have a little ceremony before letting go, naming what he is grateful for, and what he has learned from his partner and the experience of having the business.

We meet again the next week. The man who greets me at the door is beaming. "Come!" he says. He pulls me by the hand, and we tramp down the stairs together. "Look!" he says. I am amazed. The desks, the computer, the copy machine, the electronic cords, all gone. The carpet has been vacuumed, the storage area tidied, the children's costumes and toys put on shelves in plastic bins. The room is unrecognizable. There is a lightness in the area where the "office" used to be. Something lifted, in the room and inside of Ben. His hands are on his hips and a wide smile is spread across his face.

I clap my hands together. "Wow," I say. "This is really impressive."

"I can't tell you how much lighter I feel," Ben says. "There's a wonderful secondhand store right in the neighborhood that came over and picked up everything. They were thrilled. So was I. As soon as it was gone, I vacuumed the whole area. And then, I even surprised myself. I picked up the phone and called Jeff. We're getting together later this week to talk. It's been too long since we've spoken. I'm not even really nervous. It's time."

Even without additional light, the space seems to have brightened. A colorful tapestry hangs in front of the shelves in the play area, covering the plastic toy bins. A brand new giant Lego sculpture is in the middle of the open play area. The kids have definitely moved in.

"The kids have been playing down here all week. They really notice the difference. They used to tell me it was scary down here. I couldn't understand why. Without being able to name it, they could feel the weird vibes from all the old office stuff. I was oblivious."

We sit in silence, admiring the work that Ben's done and the courage it took to do the work.

"Now it's obvious to me," Ben says. "This is not the space for my office. I need to be upstairs in the light. Let me show you my new idea."

We bound up the stairs together.

TAKEAWAY

It doesn't matter where you start. Pick one thing, anything. Dust something off, move a painting to a different wall, give away some books. Wherever you start, the process seems to kick open a door, let some fresh air in a window.

Clearing stuff in the physical world opens possibility in all realms—physical, mental, emotional, and spiritual. There's an invisible thread that holds the fabric of all things together, and when you pull on it, everything rearranges itself. Try it.

As many times as I've coached about this, spoken to audiences about this, and written about it, I'm still delighted and surprised when I give away a bag of old clothes, or clear out my files, and bingo, something shifts. Like magic.

Start with something small. Listen for what wants to be cleared. Follow the thread. Be delighted by where it leads you.

Chapter Four

Listen for Your Voice

When we stop, quiet our minds, slow down the whirlwinds that are our lives, we can hear the voice that knows. It is the voice of our truth. It does not manipulate, coerce, or judge. It is not hurried, impatient, or critical. It is a gentle voice, there for us when we are ready to listen. We have to come to it. It does not come to us.

Train yourself to listen for it, which may take some practice. When confusion wraps itself around you, breathe. Let the tendrils slowly fall away. Beneath the tangle of thoughts, sitting patiently at your center, is the clear voice you are seeking. Quiet yourself and listen for that.

When you become frustrated by all the things you think you should be, do, and have, let yourself pause. Go deeper. Is this what you want, or somebody else's idea of what you should want?

Listen for your voice. It will free you from the shoulds.

It will lead you deeper and deeper into the place that is your most authentic self.

MY LESSON

Expert Opinions

My doctor calls me from her cell phone on her way out of town for a long weekend. "You have breast cancer," she says with no tender preamble. There's a lot of static on the line. The reception fades in and out. My mind goes blank. I'm standing in the living room on a late summer afternoon, barefoot, wearing shorts and a T-shirt, the phone in my left hand. I stare at the pumpkin walls, the hardwood floors, I stare at the phone. I'm in free fall.

"Call my office," she says in an everyday voice, "and schedule a lumpectomy for next Friday." The room is spinning. I hold tight to the corner of the couch.

I don't cry right away. The words inch their way like a lazy turtle from my brain to my body. When they finally register in my body, I explode. I throw down the phone, grab a pillow from the couch, and smash my head into it, over and over. I wrap my arms tight around my waist, clutch my body close, and convulse with tears.

"Call her office," she said. "Schedule the surgery," she said. "Make the appointment for next Friday." All clear thoughts fall out of my head. I bow to my doctor's orders. I become weak in the knees. Suddenly life is a fast-moving train, hurtling into a dark tunnel.

After a weekend of tears, too many phone calls, too

much hand-wringing, I exhaust myself. Emptied by so much crying, my mind begins to quiet.

"Stop," a voice in my head says. "This is *your* body. Make this work for you. Listen to the experts, but don't put them in charge."

I take some time, get quiet, and check in with my body and with my heart. I am supposed to leave Philly for Los Angeles in three days to spend two weeks with my family. I really want and need the time with them. My parents aren't well, I miss my daughters, I miss my sisters. Maybe the surgery can wait?

I make a few phone calls to other doctor friends and find that some types of breast cancer are relatively slow growing. The surgery can wait a few weeks. I write a little speech, rehearse it several times, and call my doctor. I tell her I want to go to California and push the surgery out by three weeks. I expect a fight. Instead she agrees with me and says some people want to get it over as soon as possible. She gives me her blessing. I am winning my body back.

It's a smart choice, a lucky choice. Once the cancer treatment begins, it lasts a year, during which I'm unable to travel—except back and forth to the smorgasbord of doctors.

Throughout, I keep listening to my body. It serves me well. I listen to the "experts," and I consult my body. Sometimes they agree. Sometimes not. When they agree, I'm most grateful, when they contradict each other, I thank the experts for their wisdom and choose to follow my own sage advice.

I can't make the cancer go away, but I can choose

how to be with it while it's here. And that makes all the difference.

JOCELYN

Fabric of Happiness

Jocelyn cut her teeth in the sixties. She marched on Washington, let her thick hair go long and wild, started a food collective, wore ripped jeans, tie-dyed shirts, and spent a night or two in jail. She was a hippie, an activist, and a feminist.

Time passed. She married, had children, cut her hair, and upscaled her clothes, but continued to hold fast to her social justice values.

"We stood for something in the sixties. We had a vision, a world that included everyone. Women counted, blacks counted. We were willing to speak out, march, even go to jail. There was a vitality to our lives," Jocelyn says. "I've lost that vitality. I don't know what matters to me anymore."

Jocelyn's primary job is chief financial officer for an interior design firm. In addition, she maintains a few private bookkeeping clients, is involved in local and national elections, is host to charitable fund-raisers, has neighborhood potluck gatherings, and keeps her husband and four grown children in line. She is not really sure why she called me. What she does know is that she works too hard, avoids her husband, and doesn't exercise. Everything feels heavy. Her voice is angry and tight.

"Let's start with what does matter to you," I say. "Let's see what we can discover."

"My house matters to me. I love my house," she says. "But it's buried under so much stuff I can't even appreciate it. Sewing matters to me, creating handbags from scraps of fabric matters to me. I love creating beauty, in many forms."

She wants to start with her house. A three-story New England colonial with a gracious oak front door, original maple staircase and banisters, crown molding in the living room and dining room, beveled transoms in the windows. A house with character and presence. Her adult children have moved on, leaving empty bedrooms aching to be transformed.

"Pick a room," I say. "We don't even know exactly what we're looking for yet. But you have a feeling it's buried somewhere in the house."

Jocelyn chooses the green room, the guest room. It is the physical mirror to Jocelyn's inner chaos. Crammed between the walls are a television, broken treadmill, a sewing table buried under boxes of dress-up clothes, plastic containers of art supplies, financial books, a basket overflowing with mending, bags and bags of scrap fabric, and two partially functioning sewing machines behind the TV. There's no way to get from one end of the room to the other. A yellow spool of thread sits on top of the television set. This is where we begin.

"Talk to me about sewing," I say. A pair of good pinking shears, a measuring tape, and some marking chalk sit on the side table.

Jocelyn's face lights up. "Oh, the handbags. I make them for fun. I love designing, finding bits and pieces of fabric to line and decorate. It makes me so happy. But I hardly ever sew. It seems so trivial. It has no value— it doesn't make a difference in the bigger scheme of things. Think about it: making handbags versus being a social justice activist. It's a little embarrassing. I kind of keep it a secret," she says.

We are sitting in the green room. Three bags lay atop the television. They are works of art, fabric layered on fabric, designs and colors. Jocelyn loves things that are well crafted and have attention to detail. A small voice begs her to listen. She wants a place where she can work on her creations, a place where she can display and admire them. It's a challenge to admit to herself that she has a passion for making women's purses. She identifies strongly as a political activist, a women's rights activist. She doesn't discuss her sewing life. There is no space in her mind for such a contradiction. There is no space in her home. So she muffles the voice.

"Talk to me about people who make handbags," I say. "What does it mean to you? What does it say about who you are?"

"Handbags are shallow. It's about image, not substance. They have no value. Our world is filled with serious challenges. Global warming, racism, hunger, poverty. I can't sit around making handbags when there are real problems to address. I mean really!" she says.

As we talk, she notices her less-than-generous attitude about people who make handbags. The story she tells herself goes something like this: The world needs saving, and it is up to a conscious few to dedicate their lives to the cause. Everything else is frivolous and should take a backseat until the world has been saved. She clenches her teeth, is perpetually annoyed with her husband, resents her children, and snaps at her co-workers. The voice that pushes her to save the world is harsh and unrelenting. Her own small voice, which whispers to her to create beauty, has been ignored. When she begins to notice the cost of not listening, things begin to shift.

"Let's clear out the green room so that we can have a space for guests, use the treadmill, and watch TV. But this isn't going to be the place for my sewing. I want my own space. Come look at this room, and tell me what you think," she says and walks me down the hall to a six-by-eight-foot room that has been used for storage.

"Perfect," I say.

It's filled with boxes, a broken suitcase, old books ready to be given away. A long window overlooks her vegetable garden. There is not an inch of floor space.

"Yes," she says, "perfect."

She spends several days clearing out the room: bags to be donated, clothes, books, and random stuff for her kids to cart away, the broken suitcase to toss. Her own voice is a little louder, a little clearer. She is happy clearing. She is making a space for herself. She sets up a card table for her sewing machine, organizes all her fabric by color, puts it in plastic bins, and places it on the shelves. She displays the completed handbags on the back wall.

It doesn't happen all at once. Each time I come

over she shows me something new. A pair of pants finally mended, a Halloween costume for a queen. She starts saying, "I'm making room for my vitality." She is listening to her own voice. She smiles more. She is less angry with her husband. They start having weekly date nights. She starts using the treadmill and packing a lunch for work.

"Davia, I want to ask you a work question. One of my staff whines a lot. She doesn't do her work and drags herself around the office complaining about everything. I've tried ignoring her. I've tried avoiding her. I've tried humoring her. I tried everything but telling her the truth. I don't know how to have a straightforward conversation with her. I'm worried that if we fire her, she won't be able to find another job. In the meantime, she's not doing her job and she's making me and everyone else crazy," Jocelyn says. "I want to tell her the truth. Can you help me find the right words and the right voice?"

The more time Jocelyn spends in her sewing room, creating a space for herself, listening to her own voice, the more she appreciates the importance of others' finding their own voices. Some thread connects the two in a mysterious way. The more time she spends in her sewing room, the more she wants to support others in finding their own sewing rooms.

"It's funny," she tells me. "The more I do things that make me happy, the easier it is for me to notice that Irene is not happy, and I'm not doing her any favors by not telling her the truth. I realized I knew what to do, even without your advice. I sat down with her and said,

'You're not happy here, and we're are not happy when you are not happy. For everybody's well-being, here's what we need from you: Show up and be part of the team, or look for work that makes you smile. We want the best for you. It may not be here.'

"Davia, the conversation flowed. It was easy to tell the truth. I had myself as a model, and that made a big difference. I watched myself shift gears and start doing what makes me happy instead of what I thought I was supposed to be doing, and I saw what a difference it made for me and everyone around me. I felt confident giving her the same permission. Irene decided to leave the job. She didn't go away mad. She went away with blessings from the rest of the staff. It was exhilarating to be part of a process that was so clean and truthful."

"Jocelyn, you rock!" I say. "Remember the person who came to me several months ago, with a crowded house, a furrowed brow, an angry voice. You just had a brilliant conversation with a staff member. You can bet that she'll remember this conversation for a long time. You gave her the room she needed to find something that is more suited to her. Next time, she may be able to ask for what she wants rather than walking around with such a long, sour face. One step at a time, right?"

Jocelyn hired a new staff member, someone who was excited to be part of the team. She didn't settle. It made everyone's life a little sweeter.

Saving the world and making handbags started as a contradiction. Irreconcilable. But as Jocelyn listened to her own voice, and followed what gave her joy, she infused the rest of her life with a new vitality. Political action wasn't quite as heavy. Social justice not quite as grim. There was more room for others to follow their own voice, making a little bit more room for peace in the world.

CASSANDRA

Words of Validation

Cassandra is an artist. She is a dancer, a singer, a poet. She wears layers of diaphanous fabric, silver bangles up her arms, and ribbons in her hair.

It's hard to characterize the type of work she does. It doesn't fit neatly into any particular category. She is called shaman, teacher, guide. She works with women, with students, with communities, to create rituals, produce events, guide transitions. She uses movement, chanting, silence, and drawing as she works.

Though her work may be considered unconventional, her marketing strategy is not. Most of her clients find her through her website. Her challenge is to design a website with copy and images that reflect who she is and how she works.

"I'm stuck," she says. "I've written copy for my website, but it's clunky and dense. Not at all the feeling I want to convey. I know it's wrong, but I don't know how to make it right. It's hard to find words for something so ephemeral, and without the right words it's difficult to market myself."

The copy and design of her website contradict each other. The design, in earthy tones, is clean and refreshing. The words, however, go on for pages, include too much of everything, and have no focal point. The voice is stiff and removed. There is palpable tension between the two voices.

When I look at the website, I can see an astonishing unconventional healer hungry for conventional legitimacy. The vibrant background matches Cassandra's energy. It is alive, eye-catching—healing, even. However, when I read the copy, I don't find Cassandra's lightness in the words: "Cassandra is a multitalented practitioner, highly trained in a variety of modalities, with vast experience as a teacher and guide." It certainly doesn't capture her spirit. It seems as if she is trying to impress someone, but not someone who is likely to be a client.

"Cassandra, when you look at the website, what catches your eye, and what makes you grimace? Who is this website talking to?" I ask.

"It's all twisted inside of me," she tells me. "There is this push-pull. I feel like I need to look and sound a certain way to be taken seriously, that I need a degree from an important school, a tailored hairdo, and big formal words. But then, that's not me, and that's not who I want to attract. But the legitimacy thing is really strong. Since I don't have that degree, I put all these extra words in my bio to sound as if I know what I'm talking about. And then it doesn't sound like me anymore. Ugh, this is hard. The thing is, I do know what I'm talking about. I'm an amazing healer and teacher."

"Cassandra, I hear this story so often. Many of my clients are unconventional. They are trailblazers, rule-breakers, pioneers. They color outside the lines, as do I. Even so, we all have a loud need and desire to be seen as legitimate for the work we do. We might not get it from the powers that be. We have to find legitimacy within ourselves. Internal legitimacy, rather than external legitimacy. I didn't say it would be easy."

We are sitting cross-legged on the carpeted floor of my office. A scented candle is burning. The computer is open to her website. In the corner of the page is a photo of Cassandra twirling inside a gauzy shawl. She is grinning from ear to ear. Her black skirt comes to mid-calf and her bare feet are raised slightly off the ground.

"Let's go over the copy," I suggest. "Starting with your bio. What do you want people to know about you? I don't mean details like where you went to school. What do you want them to know about who you are at your essence? About your spirit?"

Cassandra's black hair is tied back away from her face with a long red ribbon. She is in perpetual motion, swaying to music I can't hear. Humming quietly. A small, dark green stone hangs from a silver chain around her neck.

She smiles. "I hear music, I hear the music of other people's bodies. People move in my presence, they sway and laugh, and things fall away when we dance together. It is hard to put words to my work. The work is in the body, not in the mind."

"That sounds good to me. Your work is not for everyone. Draw the people who want to hear what you are saying. Your legitimacy has to start with you. When you speak in your true voice, you express your own legitimacy. That's all you need."

She takes some time to rewrite the copy. We come back together the next week.

"Now look," she says. We're back on the floor of my office. Computer open to her website. She is grinning. She clicks on the bio page and begins to read. "Shaman, teacher, healer ... "

"Wow!" I say. "You nailed it. The words and pictures go together and you come shining through. Your distinct voice is right there. How does that feel? Talk to me about legitimacy."

"Something definitely shifted. I'm so proud. When I got to the essence of me, I didn't feel like I needed to embellish in any way. My truth is big enough, legitimate enough. That legitimacy issue may come back again, in some other form, but for now we sure took a big bite out of it," she says.

She stands up and starts dancing around the room, her arms out wide, she's twirling, her head back, laughing. "I am who I am. This is what you get. What a trip."

Respecting the Artist

"I might look like I don't care what people think, with my tattoos and my funky hair, but the truth is I care a lot. In certain ways, I'm driven by what others think; I just look like I'm an artiste," Amelia says.

Amelia is an independent filmmaker in her midthirties, raised in a family of scientists and intellectuals, all of whom have doctorates from prestigious universities. They have been widely published, and their office walls are papered with commendations. She wrestles with her choice to pursue filmmaking, feeling she is falling short of family expectations.

With several award-winning short films already in distribution, she decided to go back to school for a master's degree in film, hoping the academic degree would quiet the noise in her head. Her passion is social change, and film is her medium. Her first film, a call to action for climate change, toured the country with a noted film festival. She is smart, talented, creative— able to take a challenging, controversial subject and tell a story that informs, and unites people to make change. But she is not united within herself. She demeans her film work, calling it insignificant because it's not based in academia, the god under which she was raised.

"I may carry myself as a pioneer, a change agent,

but inside I'm a failed academic, someone who should have majored in biology, gotten a PhD, and pursued climate change as a scientist, not as a filmmaker, heaven forbid. I keep asking myself, what does Amelia want? I don't know. I don't know. I can't hear my own voice because the voices of my parents are so loud. That's the question I want to answer in our coaching: What does Amelia want?"

"Our goal is to provide enough quiet in your head for you to be able to distinguish the various voices," I say. "And to be able to hear them objectively, to discover what each has to say without the judgment you have piled on top of them."

Amelia tells me that her parents were in their twenties when they emigrated from Russia. They set the bar high, valued formal education, and expected Amelia to follow their example. While she values many of the things her parents value—family and social justice issues—her learning has taken place in more unconventional ways.

"Talk to me about making films. What turns you on, what gets you excited?" I ask.

"Global warming is real," she says. "This moment in history is filled with opportunity. We can come together, put aside our pettiness, and come up with solutions that will matter to the entire planet. Or we can close our eyes, go numb, and pretend like someone else is in charge. That's not the way I want to play. I get excited by the possibilities, the dreaming that has to happen, the forgiveness, and the generosity. And film is my medium. I love creating the vision, using image, sound, and story to motivate people. I love the whole process."

We're sitting in my office, in slouchy chairs, our shoes off. She is beaming, her breathing deep and steady.

"It is so refreshing to listen to you talk about making films and your commitment to issues of climate. You light up when you speak. Are you aware of that? Tell me what it feels like in your body? Who is speaking now?" I ask.

I ask Amelia to sit with the feeling for a few moments before she answers.

"I feel alive, sparkly, on top of my game. I wish I could carry this feeling with me all the time wherever I am, in whatever I'm doing. It feels right. This is me, this is my voice," she says.

"We're going to switch gears and listen to some of the other voices in your head. It's important that you listen to what they are saying," I say. "Let's talk about academia, credibility, and prestige. Talk to me about who you think you are supposed to be, about who you think your parents want you to be."

Her shoulders rise, she pulls her legs closer in, and she wraps her arms around her waist. A bit of spirit drains from Amelia's body. An entirely new person appears before me.

This is a wrestling place for me as well. My own path has been circuitous, looping back on itself, collecting wisdom through my crazy life experiences, push-pulling against the mainstream, the status quo, resisting the fancy degrees and any well-defined occupation. Over time my own voice has become clearer and more distinct, but it is challenging to go against the grain. I turn to the courageous heroes and heroines in my own life, to remind me that cutting my own path is worth the effort. As I sit with Amelia, my heart aches for her. She will make her own choices. The best I can do is offer my big listening.

"My parents say I should live my own life, make my own choices, but I can't help but think that I'm disappointing them by not getting an advanced degree in biology or political science. Film just seems, well, so lightweight, not substantial enough. It's true, it's my issue, not theirs. I'm the one who is saying that filmmaking is not worthy. I am an artist living in a culture that doesn't recognize the value of art. I'm an outsider wanting in. An outsider pushing away the straight and narrow life. It makes me crazy," she says.

Amelia is driven. She is a doer—as a student and as a filmmaker. She is in constant motion. She has turned her filmmaking into work, pushing herself to produce and complete her projects. The artist, the internal, playful, creative spirit, the one who meanders toward no goal, has been shoved to the corner, buried under the to-do list, and the manufactured urgency of life.

"Let's find a way to invite the artist out to play," I suggest. "Nothing fancy like making a movie, just some doodles, some kid stuff. Tell me what that might look like."

"I love it when I sit at a table filled with big pieces of paper, crayons, acrylics, glue, scissors, and just let myself draw and cut and glue. It's very relaxing. Nothing has to be perfect, I don't even have to keep what I make. I start to quiet down in my head. Things lose their urgency and importance. I have fun! And then that sense of fun carries over into everything else I do," she says.

"Let's take a look at your schedule. How do you spend your time? Do you make time for doodling?" I ask.

She tells me her schedule. She is booked with classes, meetings, plans, social time, and filmmaking day and night. I'm exhausted just listening to her. She enjoys her friendships and her colleagues, but spending too much time around people drains her. Amelia is a person who wants and needs time alone to recharge.

"If you were to rearrange your schedule to include more artist time, more recharge time, what would it look like?" I ask.

"I'd flip it so that I'm home five nights a week and go out on two, rather than the other way around. I'd set aside two of the home nights for special time, time to spin in circles, lay on the couch doing nothing, play with colored pencils, time to let the night unfold without plan or directive," she says.

When we talk after two weeks of this new schedule, she's ecstatic. "It's like a small miracle," she says. "When we started this conversation it was about artist versus academic, a battleground of two strong and opposing forces. And in that fight nobody was winning—not unlike the climate conversation. In listening for my own voice, I've found a way to respect the artist *and* the academic. I discovered it doesn't have to be either or. Integrating the two makes my work even stronger."

TAKEAWAY

"Be yourself, everyone else is already taken."
– OSCAR WILDE

We are surrounded by voices that tell us to do this, be that. Voices that tell us we're not enough, we should be different, we're too loud, odd, strange, weird, demanding. Some of those voices come from the outside; most, it turns out, come from within ourselves.

It takes energy to fight against them, and it's noisy. Stop fighting. Get quiet and listen. Sense the resonance of the unique, exceptional, particular human pulse that is you. It takes an act of courage to live that life.

Listen for your own voice. Tune your ears, tune your body, tune your soul. Follow your voice. At first you may not recognize it, you may even reject it. Be patient. It will get stronger, louder, more vibrant. Follow your voice. Follow it for your own sake. Follow it for the rest of us hungry for courageous leadership. The world will be richer because of your authentic presence.

Chapter Five

Ask for Support

A child asks the difference between heaven and hell. A wise soul answers:

HELL is a room with a large round table. In the middle of the table is a simmering pot of stew. It smells delicious. The people sitting around the table are thin and sickly. They are holding spoons with very long handles strapped to their arms. They reach into the pot of stew with their spoons, but because the handle is longer than their arms, they can't get the spoons back into their mouths. They are famished. Their eyes are dull. Their hearts are parched.

HEAVEN is a room with a large round table. In the middle of the table is a simmering pot of stew. It smells delicious. The people sitting around the table are holding spoons with very long handles strapped to their arms. They reach into the pot of stew with their spoons, turn toward each other and feed one another. They are well nourished. They are laughing and talking. Their eyes shine. Their hearts are full.

Asking for support does not come easy. We do not readily admit that we need each other, that we are scared, that we can't do it alone. We want to believe we are invincible and always have the upper hand. The price we pay for this attitude is isolation and loneliness. When we put down our armor and ask for support something altogether unexpected happens. We connect at the most authentic level of self and learn to cherish our vulnerability rather than run from it.

The Power of Surrender

I'm not used to asking for help. I'm an oldest child. My first words must've been, "I can do it myself." But when the cancer comes I can't.

The chemo has me laid out. Walking from the living room to the dining room is heroic. I sit most of the day in a big old chair moved from the living room into the kitchen while friends cook, clean, and chat. The phone rings. When I make a move to answer it, a friend motions me to stay put. I am so used to being in charge, being in control. Harder than the cancer is surrendering to my vulnerability.

Holding the phone in her hand, my friend looks in my direction. I shake my head and sink back into the chair.

"She's very grateful you called. She's too tired to talk—can you call back in a few days?" my friend says.

I want so desperately to please everyone, I don't want to let anyone down. They want to support me, listen to my story, ask me questions, and I have no energy.

I let others take care of me. It's hard. I feel so vulnerable. I am vulnerable. I'm moved by the generosity of the people in my life. Something in me cracks open. I practice being taken care of, asking for support. People want to help. They want to matter.

Another friend organizes meals, signs people up to cook, and deliver dinners to me. I don't even have the energy to protest. I am not used to this attention. I don't want to share this broken, bald, needy part of myself. I want to hide myself away and not reemerge until my hair returns and I am all stitched together again. But I can't do this alone.

I learn something surprising: In my broken state, I connect more deeply with the brokenness in others. We hold one another up, and find comfort in doing so. I keep practicing asking for support. Some days are better than others.

I am healthy now. All my body parts work. My energy is restored. However, in my healthy state I don't always feel the same permission to ask for help, thinking I should be able to manage my life on my own. I am grateful when something from my past gives me a little nudge, reminding and encouraging me to reach out. I keep rediscovering that my life is so much lighter and fuller when I let others support me. And that people want to help. They want to feel needed. Asking for support is a real sign of my health.

SANDY

A Taxing Situation

Three years ago, Sandy opened a neighborhood café with the vision that it would be a gathering place for readings, visionary speakers, and social networking opportunities. She is smart, ambitious, and committed to global change through community participation. She has lived in this neighborhood for fifteen years and watched as new businesses have opened and flourished. The café is a demonstration of commitment to her community's improvement. She is in her late thirties, lives with her partner Julia and their preschool-age daughter, Lucy. Colorful clothing is her signature— turquoise scarves; red shoes; orange, yellow, and blue caftans; silver bangles; always a visual delight for customers when they walk in the door of the café.

On the surface, life looks good. The café is crowded. The poetry readings are a success. Lucy's preschool is engaging and creative. Julia loves her work at the university. But beneath the surface, a hairline fissure is threatening to split wide open.

"I owe three years in back taxes, with big penalties coming up. There's a chunk of work to be done, and I need someone to hold me accountable," Sandy says. "I'm hoping you are that person. Hannah gave me your name. She said you never made her feel bad about anything. I can hardly talk about this. I need to work with someone who will be gentle and still hold me to my word. There's paperwork, data entry, people to call, reports to be filed. It's all crazy-making. Every time I think about it, I want to go to sleep."

Sandy is tired and anxious. She doesn't get enough sleep. Her staff is fidgety. She spends less and less time with her daughter, family time is almost nonexistent, and time with Julia has fallen off the calendar altogether.

A call from the IRS marks a turning point. The one she is unconsciously waiting for. The one that doesn't look anything like what she thinks she is waiting for. Yet it is this piece of news that opens up Sandy, that pushes her to ask for help.

The woman who calls me has already cracked open. She feels shame and embarrassment. She feels stupid and irresponsible. But she knows that three years of neglected taxes are a metaphor for a larger picture.

Her café is a gathering spot, a place to share, to support, to enjoy one another's company—something she desperately wants for herself in her personal life. But her "I can do it myself" attitude has left her in isolation. She often gets home after Lucy is asleep. After Julia is asleep. They lead full and separate lives—not what they intended when they first got together.

We examine the tax situation. There are many entangled components. Her relationship with her accountant, gathering necessary records, data entry, conversations with Julia. It is just big enough, just tangled enough to require a team effort. What a gift. Sandy is about to get practice asking for support, help, and partnership—all more challenging, it turns out, than opening a café.

She has a tangible goal and timeline for our coaching work. She wants me to help her think strategically, create a task list, and hold her accountable. I suspect that once we open the books, we'll discover a wealth of underlying issues, but our immediate task is clear.

"Let's start by taking all the pieces out of your head and put them on paper. You'll begin to breathe more easily. Start by telling me what you know. Once we have the picture, we can see whether anything is missing and what steps need to be taken," I say.

We're doing this coaching over the phone. Sandy is at the café, upstairs in her office, she tells me, where her desk overlooks the narrow street, the apex of the neighborhood. It is spring. Apple and pear blossoms line the street. Her office is small and tidy. Voices can be heard from the café downstairs. The smell of coffee and pastries fills the air, she tells me. A photo of Lucy and Julia sits on her desk. A fortune from a fortune cookie is tacked to her bulletin board; it reads, "You will be successful in matters of business and family."

She tells me about her workdays, and it is immediately apparent that Sandy is a one-woman show. She drops her daughter at preschool early in the morning and is at the café before the doors open. She sweeps the floors and micromanages the staff. She is the last one out at night. Even with a staff of five at the café, she tries to do it all herself. She is heroic, or at least that's how she views herself. Asking for help, even asking for partnership, is not in her vocabulary. Strong, smart women fly solo, she believes. Her unspoken operating principle is, "I can do it myself, I don't need anyone else's help."

This is in direct contradiction to the philosophy of the café. But sometimes a strong contradiction creates tension that can break the old pattern and open the way for new, more useful behavior.

"I have an accountant, a bookkeeper, and a café manager. My accountant is slow to return my phone calls. The bookkeeper is unreliable. He says he's going to show and doesn't," she complains. "My manager is good, but I find myself watching over everything she does. It's all very time-consuming, not to mention frustrating."

"Let's create a list of tasks, prioritize them, and set due dates," I suggest.

Data entry is a high priority. Sandy's first job is to contact Bill, the bookkeeper, and set times for him to come in. Nothing can move forward until he completes his part.

"Until now you've relied only on yourself. You assumed other people would let you down, and you didn't call them out or ask them to rise to the occasion," I say. "To create partnership you need to be clear about what you want, hold others accountable, and trust that they can do what you expect. You've let Bill slide in the past, and when he didn't show up you didn't complain. If you want to be able to rely on him, he needs to know that you mean business," I say.

An empty water bottle sits on my desk. My pen sits uncapped on my notepad. I ask Sandy to practice having this conversation with Bill, to experiment with words and tones of voice to convey the seriousness of her intent without being critical or patronizing.

"Ugh, I hate doing this. I feel so stupid. I feel like you don't trust me," she says.

"Here's another perspective," I say. "A well-known poet is coming to speak at the café, and you will be introducing her. You want the introduction to be clear and strong and reflect your admiration for her work. Before she arrives, you write and rewrite the piece and practice speaking it until it feels natural. You want to be prepared and appropriate with your remarks. The same goes for Bill. In your past communications with him, you asked him to come in to work on the books, he said he would and then didn't follow through. That's useful feedback. Something needs to shift in the way you're asking him to show up. It might feel awkward at first. Give it a shot."

She's embarrassed, but gives it a try. "Hi, Bill, it's Sandy. Can you come in to the café on Monday or Tuesday to finish up the books?"

"Give yourself some feedback. What works and what doesn't work about your request?" I ask.

"I asked him straight out to come finish the books, but I wasn't really that specific about when, and I didn't stress the urgency. It seemed like a casual request," she says.

"Good noticing. Try it again and make the changes you think would make it a more powerful request," I say.

"Bill, this is Sandy. I really need your support in

finishing the books. We need to have everything complete in two weeks. That means I need you to do your part this week. Let's schedule three two-hour blocks of time for this week so that I can be assured that the books will be done on time," she says.

"Wow! What did that feel like?" I ask.

"It was kind of exhilarating! It felt so easy because I wasn't trying to beat around the bush. I just came straight out and said what I needed. Thank you for making me do this exercise. I didn't want to, but now I see the value. I'm totally ready to call him now," she says. "I'm even excited. I get it now about my attitude, my words, and my tone of voice. He needs to show up, and I need to be able to count on him. It's not complicated."

Sandy calls me the next week. "Bill finished the books! I called him and asked in very much the same voice I used with you. I could tell that he heard me. He kept his word and did everything he said he would do. I'm so delighted—not only that the books are done, but I really learned something about asking and being willing to let people help me," she says.

"Way to go!" I say.

"This has really opened a door for me. I never noticed how much I needed to control everything. I don't want to operate like that anymore. It may not happen overnight, but I'd like to talk about ways that I can entrust others with more responsibility. Starting with the event planning. I've been researching and booking all the events for the café. I think I'm ready to let my manager take that over. That would take a huge load off my shoulders, give me more time with my family, and let my manager know that I trust her to get the job done," she says.

In coaching, I want to draw on Sandy's wisdom. She learned a lot in her interaction with Bill. Now she gets to take that knowledge and apply it to the next opportunity.

As we continue to work together, she slowly gives away more and more to her capable staff. Lucy is happy. Julia is happy. And Sandy finds something delightful in her dream café—it doesn't simply support its community, it is a community that can support her. That didn't come about the way she imagined, but no matter. In the end, everybody wins.

CASEY
The Group Show

"I'm really scared, but I want to organize an exhibit of my artwork, and maybe include a few other artists. I have this idea of how I want to do it, but I don't really know what to do," Casey says.

Casey is a collage artist, filmmaker, and musician. She is recognized in the art community for her bold, distinct style. But away from the canvas, she is tentative, doesn't fit well in her body, keeps her head turned down, and speaks as if she doesn't want to disturb the air around her. It took an act of courage for her to pick up the phone to call me. Asking for support is miles outside of her comfort zone.

"Tell me more about what you want for this show and how you want me to support you," I say.

We sit at an outdoor café table, a striped awning shading us from the summer heat. She stares at the table and twirls a spoon between her fingers, making lazy circles next to her glass of iced tea. Her knees bump up against the underside of the table. Even in the heat, she wears her black pants, black T-shirt, black Converse sneakers. Her short, cropped black hair completes the picture.

"I'm not very good at planning or making lists or follow-through or asking people for things. I want to have the show, but I don't know how to put all the pieces together. Maybe you could help me think about how to do this and make it real," she says.

She is doodling on her napkin.

"You have a goal, to have an exhibit of your artwork. You've told me that your vision of the opening-night reception is a gallery filled with your work and the work of several other collaborating artists. There are guests smiling and crowding in to get a closer look, critics with their pens and cameras, and you standing proudly by, a witness to your artist self. This is not just about hanging your art. This is something that will stretch you big time, pull you forward, build muscles you never thought you had. In the end, the exhibit will be the celebration and culmination of months of work and training. It is your opportunity to step forward, as an artist, as a human being. Is this what you want to sign up for?" I ask.

The doodles now cover her entire napkin, filling it with exploding stars, exclamation points, and thought bubbles. Casey's foot is swinging back and forth under the table. Her iced tea glass is empty.

She looks up. "This is exactly what I want to sign up for," she says.

She sets a date for the exhibit, giving herself six months to put the whole thing together. Together we create a vision and a timeline, and begin to identify all the tasks and their completion dates. The project is a big one, not one that can be done alone.

"I want three or four other artists to collaborate with me, but I don't know who I want to ask. I don't know—I can't think of anyone else who would really want to put this together with me. It seems like I'd be asking too much," she says.

Casey's first challenge was simply letting herself want something at all. Asking for what she wants is challenge number two. We begin to practice. She is developing a new muscle. The ask muscle. It's important to start with a request that is the right weight, not too light, not too heavy. Something that will create a stretch, but not so big that it will create a break. We look for that.

"Tell me about the artists in your life. Are there people you already work with? People you feel safe with? People you admire?" I ask over the phone.

Casey is in her bedroom, lying on her bed, her cat curled next to her. Discarded clothes are piled on the floor next to the bed, art pieces in progress tacked to the walls. A long, wide desk in the corner of the bedroom serves as her studio.

"I have three artist friends that I'd like to get together with for a casual art night. We could meet somewhere to work on our own projects, and we'd have each other's company, and it would give us a bit of structure. I'm nervous to invite them though," she says.

"Choose one of the three people. Let's have a practice conversation. We're starting here with a small request. We're going to build your ask muscles," I say.

"OK, I'll start with Steven. We've worked on some projects together before. I know he likes me and he likes my work. We've even talked about having an exhibit before. I think he might be interested in getting together once a week," she says.

"What do you want to ask him?"

"I want to tell him, 'I'm putting together a weekly art night. I know you're really busy and you might not want to do this, but do you think you might want to show up once in a while?' I guess I'd say something like that," she says.

"Let's forget about Steven for a moment. Just talk to me. In your wildest dreams, what would you like from him, how often do you want him to show up, how seriously do you want him to consider your invitation?" I ask.

It's quiet on the phone. Not wanting is safer than wanting and not getting. Not asking is safer than asking and having someone say no. There is power in learning how to ask. Even when the answer is no.

"I want him to take it seriously. I want him to want to come and to show up every week on time and to stay for three hours and to feel grateful for our time together. That is in my wildest dreams. But I don't think I can really ask for that. That's too big a request," she says.

"What you just said to me is very clear. Say it again, but direct it toward Steven."

"Steven, I'm organizing a weekly art night at my house. My idea is a three-hour get-together with two or three other people, and we support each other to do our art. You are one of the first people I thought of. Would you be interested in being part of Casey's art night?" she says.

"Wow, that felt really good!" she says. "It's actually almost easier to just come right out and say what you want than to dance around it."

She continues to practice until the words feel easy. By the time she talks to Steven, her tone has shifted from shuffling apology to something that borders on opportunity. Steven is thrilled with the idea and says yes immediately.

She asks Natalie, who says no, she's too busy. Marcus hears about it from Steven and asks whether he can be invited to art night. Natalie tells Grace, who says yes. Casey never even considered asking Grace; that she would want to come is beyond Casey's wildest dreams.

Making a clear request for friends to join her in weekly art nights is Casey's first practice at asking for what she wants. Over the next six months, she finishes a body of work, asks her art night buddies to collaborate with her on the exhibit, books a gallery, and asks other friends to cater and photograph the event.

On opening night, the gallery is filled with art from five artists, smiling guests nibbling on hors d'oeuvres, cameras clicking, and a beaming Casey taking it all in. The gallery is an external demonstration of her inner stretch. Casey's comfort zone is wider and broader, her ability to ask and receive expanded. Six months ago, she held herself back, not wanting to ask, feeling like an intruder. Today, she sees the gift she has to share, and she's become someone who creates a space for people to share their art.

RHEA

Interviews

Rhea is tall and lanky. She wears jeans, a T-shirt, and a cap backward over her short brown hair. Sunglasses cover her eyes. She prefers not to be called a woman. In her midthirties, she has been making films for more than ten years.

She likes being behind the camera, invisible, not wanting to call attention to herself. She has spent most of her life trying to please others, trying to fit in. It isn't working. She feels like a man trapped in a woman's body, making it hard to go unnoticed. She is working on a documentary film about gender—searching for a way to understand her own story. The project is too big, too scary to take on alone. She calls me. We meet to talk.

"This is how I work," I say. "We take all the stuff of your life—the circumstances, your relationships, all your interactions—and use it as information. You are coming to me because you want to finish your film project. Right now you're feeling stopped by time and money and creativity. However, as we explore, we might discover that this is not about time, or money, or creativity, but something else altogether."

I ask her questions about where she is in the filmmaking process. Where is she stuck, what's next, what kind of support does she need from me?

"I want to interview people for my film, but I don't really know who to ask, or how to ask," she says.

This is a big step. To approach others who feel out of place in their bodies is to step outside of her own invisibility. Her own story will transform in the process of asking others to tell their stories.

"What about the Gay and Lesbian Center? They might have a support group that deals with gender issues," I say.

I am listening intently to her voice over the phone. I can't see the expression on her face.

"Yes, the Gay and Lesbian Center does have a support group, but I've been too afraid to go. I don't know what I would say," Rhea tells me in her quiet, tentative voice after a long silence.

"This is your starting place," I say. "Go to a meeting. There will be others there who are just as nervous, shy, scared as you are. You don't need to say anything; your presence will be a support to them in the same way that their presence will be a support for you. You are a filmmaker, but you're also discovering your own story. Go sit in the group. I think you'll discover that there are others dealing with the same issues. That's step one. Come back and talk, and we'll see what's next."

Rhea calls me the next week. "I went to the weekly support group. There were eight people and one leader-type person. Mostly people told stories about what they're thinking and feeling. Some people were considering taking hormones, and they talked about how hard it was to make that choice. It felt good to know that other people are struggling with some of the same issues that I'm struggling with. You can't imagine how hard it is to be in a woman's body and feel like a man. I never feel like anyone really understands. But at least here I saw that there are others. I didn't feel so alone. Even so I wasn't ready to talk and slipped out when the group was over."

"Rhea, that's great that you went to the group. That was a big step. What are you thinking about for next steps?" I ask.

"I'll go back again. It feels really hard, but if I think of it as a place where I can do some research for my film it makes it easier. I'll take a deep breath and ask if anyone is willing to be interviewed," she says.

Rhea calls me after the next meeting. "I talked in the group. I told a little bit about my own story and then talked about the film. I asked if anyone wanted to be interviewed. Two people said yes," she says. "We set a time to get together. I've never really interviewed anyone before. I'm not sure what I'll ask them."

Rhea is more animated than I've ever heard her. There are very few pauses in the conversation. She plans to keep going back to the group. She says that she doesn't think anyone in the group will be her friend, but just knowing that the group is there lifts a weight from her shoulders.

"Think about what kind of questions you would want someone to ask you," I say. "That's a starting point. We could come up with a few questions so you feel more prepared, but the truth is, you may not have to ask many questions. You might just ask them to tell their story, and then let the film roll."

Mel is Rhea's first interviewee. They meet at Mel's. She tells Rhea her story. She is energetic and loves to talk. Rhea doesn't even need to encourage her. She starts the film rolling and Mel talks for an hour nonstop. She is happy to share her journey with Rhea.

"I learned so much listening to Mel. She made it really easy for me. She is not shy at all about talking. Now that I've interviewed one person, it will be a little easier to ask someone else, but Mel didn't need any prompting, so I didn't really get any practice asking questions. I guess she was a good person to start with," Rhea says.

"I want to interview Jess, but he's not much of a talker, so I'm a little concerned that it will be harder to get the information I want," she says.

"What if you ask Jess and think of it as a practice run. You can talk to him knowing it might be harder to get what you want. But after you leave him, you can think about other questions you might want to ask and then go back for a second interview. Let's come up with some questions before you even approach him so that you'll have something to go on," I suggest. "If you were going to be interviewed for a documentary, what would you want someone to ask you?"

"Hmm, that's tricky. I guess some questions about feeling invisible and not belonging and being misunderstood," she says.

"OK, how about starting with, 'Do you ever feel invisible?' Rather than assume that he feels invisible, start by finding out whether he does. If he does, then move on to asking when, and in what kinds of situations with what kinds of people. Let that lead into other questions, but if it doesn't, ask the same questions about belonging and not belonging. See where that takes you," I say.

Rhea calls me the next week. "The interview with Jess was much different from the one with Mel. Jess isn't much of a talker and neither am I. So I was really glad to have the questions. They started a conversation. There were lots of pauses and silences, but I still got some good information."

She pauses, then says, "I originally called you because I wanted to make a film about gender identity. But I was really stuck. I thought I wanted to tell other people's stories, but to do that I had to ask for their support. That was way outside of my comfort zone. It meant I had to push through my shyness and initiate some really hard conversations. Through our coaching I've learned ways to step outside of myself, and in the process of interviewing others, I discovered that it was really my own story that I wanted to tell.

"The film is almost done," she says. "It is my story. I hope others find comfort in my journey."

TAKEAWAY

Sometimes we have a vision of how we can make a difference, make a contribution. And yet going it alone is overwhelming and taxing. Some of us can ask for support—an afternoon of child care, company at a doctor's appointment—before we get to a crisis point. But many of us can't. Not until we have no other choice.

Then, unusual gifts come our way—like a call from the IRS, a diagnosis of breast cancer—and give us the opportunity to ask for what we want or need. We learn how to solicit, or just accept, support. We learn how to be part of a team. We all get bigger for it.

When we ask, we acknowledge that we are not alone, that we need one another. When we ask, we reveal our vulnerability, our fear, our shame—our raw common humanity. But we also open the door to connect with others, the essence of our strength.

Chapter Six

Pick Your Lens

There is an ancient Chinese story about a man, his plow horse, and his son. One day the man's horse runs away and the villagers moan in chorus, "We're so sorry! That's such bad news!" The man, wise and thoughtful, takes a different attitude. "Good news, bad news, who knows?" he says. Days later the horse returns with a herd of wild horses, and the villagers are jubilant. "That's such good news!" they sing in unison. Again the man refrains from judging the situation. His son, strong and steady, decides to ride one of the wild horses. When he falls and breaks his leg, the villagers are dismayed, but the man repeats his refrain, "Good news, bad news, who knows?" When the army comes later that week to conscript able-bodied men for the war, the son and his broken leg are left behind. The villagers rejoice. And the man repeats, "Good news, bad news, who knows?"

As they do to the man in the story, things happen

in our lives that we can't control. Though we cannot choose our circumstances, we do choose the attitude we hold toward them. Seeing all events through the lens of opportunity rather than the lens of crisis changes who we are.

Shifting perspective takes practice. And willingness. It requires owning our part in the situation. It doesn't make our challenges less daunting or our losses less painful. But it changes the way we understand them. It causes us to become bigger, more compassionate, and less judgmental.

It turns everything in our lives into an amazing adventure.

MY LESSON

The Final Room

It's Memorial Day weekend. The four of us sisters are in the den in the house where we grew up, the house where my parents lived for forty-seven years. We're huddled together, conspiratorially, knee-deep in photographs. Last month we moved our parents out of the house and into assisted living, my mother with Parkinson's, my dad with dementia.

We told them we were all getting together to clear out the house. They always smiled when the four sisters did anything to "improve our relationship." I'm not sure they understand that we are here at the house, or what we are doing. I try not to think about that.

Before getting to the den we went through the rest of the house. Every drawer, every closet, every box. Tagging along after one another, room after room. We put our hands on every bit of our history, touched it, caressed it, held back our tears.

My mother, before her hands began to shake, chronicled our lives with her many cameras. Her photos, just like the pencil markings on the closet doorjamb, marked our movement toward adulthood, up and up. Each trip, each celebration, each chocolate dessert gathering was captured through her lens.

We gather the photos—the framed ones from

bedrooms and hallways, the snapshots held under refrigerator magnets and tacked on the cork board— and put them in the den. We line them up against the walls, stack them on the leather couch, pile them on the oak table. The door to the den is closed against the vast emptiness of the rest of the house, the windows open to the fresh breeze. This is the final room, the end.

We're intent on getting the job done. It allows us to focus on something. For a moment we can live inside the images, pretending my mother is here chronicling us as we sort, and savor and reminisce. I'm hoping no one cries. I just keep moving.

"Where will I stay when I come to L.A.?" Eliana asks, her voice more angry than sad. What she means is: What will become of us? Who are we without this family house, this landing pad, these thick walls, and their memories? Without the place that holds this family?

Judy is sitting on the worn leather couch. Jan is on a little stool in the corner, faded photographs of my grandparents spread over her lap. A curtain rod has come away from the wall, the curtain listing to one side.

We've been losing the house for twelve years now, ever since my mother got sick. It was my mom who ran it, who breathed it alive with her photos, who kept order in the refrigerator and flowers in the garden. In the last twelve years the house has slowly gotten smaller, darker, heavier.

"Jan, take a look at this one," I say. I'm holding a black-and-white photo of Jan, standing next to her bicycle, her head down. She's sixteen. I'm eighteen.

Eliana is fourteen and Judy is eleven. We're on a family vacation in Amish country.

She hands me a photo from that same bicycle trip: me with my face in a pout, bicycle upside down by the side of the road, flat tire. My father stands at a right angle to me, his jaw clenched. The man in the picture is larger and grander than the man I know today, the one with dementia. But he's no less fierce. Now that I'm in charge of him, I try to be more generous. Sometimes I'm not.

Judy, her hair pulled back in a loose ponytail, is standing at the window, holding slides up to the light. Eliana is sorting through an envelope marked "Army days." I pick up a photo of the four of us. We're teenagers, all wearing blue work shirts and faded jeans and hair down to our waists. Jan and Eliana have light hair, fair skin. Judy and I are dark. Here we are in the den, forty years later, still in jeans, but now it is our skin that has faded. Our hair has turned gray.

I look up at my sisters. This time together in the den is precious. We live in different cities now, have complicated lives, and only see each other for holidays and special occasions.

Yes, we are saying goodbye to the house. Yes, we are slowly, slowly saying goodbye to our parents. Yet in the sadness is the simple beauty. Here we are, the four of us, together. Holding each other up. Letting each other cry. Picking up the slack when the load gets too heavy. This moment is the very thing my parents wished for—a family who was there for each other to celebrate and savor everything.

DANIEL

Not a Boat Rocker

"Davia, I have this terrible situation and I don't know how to handle it," Daniel says.

Daniel manages five people in an architectural firm. One of them, Stephen, is not pulling his weight. He is consistently late to meetings, doesn't finish projects on time, and walks around the office with a long, sour face that reads, "You can't make me."

Daniel doesn't know what to say to Stephen, or how to say it. He is a peacemaker, not a boat rocker. He likes to smooth things over. He wants everyone to get along and be happy.

For Daniel, talking to Stephen is a big, messy, no-win problem. Our work is to give Daniel a new perspective on his situation, give him more information about his own role in the matter, and open doors to a resolution that works for everyone.

"Talk to me about Stephen," I say.

"He makes me so mad," Daniel answers. "Everyone else on the team shows up to meetings on time, does really stellar work, has a good spirit, but Stephen is always whining about something. I have to go back to him several times to get work that he has promised. The weird thing is that he's really good at what he does. I respect his work as an architect. I think that makes me madder than anything. 'Just do the work,' I want to say, 'We're all counting on you.'"

At this point, I don't even suggest the potential for personal growth that this situation could provide. Daniel is too angry to be able to hear that now. We're still untangling the problem.

"He's putting me in this position. If he were acting right, I wouldn't have to say anything to him. I've bent over backward to cover for him. I make excuses to our boss, sometimes I even do his work. I never complain, I just do it because it needs to get done. If he doesn't want to be here, then why doesn't he just leave? That would make everything so much easier for all of us," Daniel admits to me.

We're sitting in the conference room of his office. Most of the staff is gone, and the building is quiet. The view from the long windows is magnificent—mountains in every direction, some dusted with snow. Flowering trees full with pink and yellow buds, billowy clouds, and a blue, blue sky. Photos of finished projects hang on the wall. It is a space conducive to creating inspired work.

"There are two things going on," I observe, "Stephen's behavior and your reaction to it. Let's separate them. First, let's look at Stephen's behavior. You have identified several specific issues of concern. He shows up late to meetings, doesn't finish his work on time, and has an attitude that affects the unity of the team. You are his boss. Your job is to give him feedback, to tell him that those behaviors don't support a good work environment," I say.

Daniel is staring out the window. He doesn't say anything.

"That's part one." I say. "Part two is your reaction to his behavior. This situation, though you've defined it as a huge problem, is actually an opportunity for you to learn something about your own behavior. This situation could become a gift. There is a place you typically stop and step back because you don't want to make waves. And my guess is that you do this in every area of your life, not just with Stephen."

The light is dancing off the mountaintops. Daniel looks up from sipping his tea.

"Oh, ugh. What you say is so true. I shy away from asking anyone for anything. I don't ask my wife, I don't ask my friends. I pretend that I'm fine and it doesn't matter, but the truth is I keep a secret tally of all the times I've gone out of my way or covered for someone. My little box of resentments. Truth is, Stephen's kind of safe. I'm mean, it's safe for me to get really mad at him because he's my co-worker—not my wife. I'm not there yet, but I'm open to the idea that this might be some kind of gift or opportunity. Wild. It's just wild."

I notice that he's almost smiling now. "So this isn't new information for you. You are reflective, and as soon as I pointed this out you knew exactly what I was talking about. What I say next probably won't surprise you either. You are very invested in being a nice guy," I observe. "You say you're covering for Stephen because you're a nice guy. Consider another possibility. Maybe you do that because you're afraid of conflict, you're afraid people won't like you." I let the words hang in the air. I want Daniel to sit with them for a few moments. Though these words may not surprise him, they may not be easy to hear.

"Oh god, it's so true. I can't stand it when people get mad at each other. Or even when they think about getting mad at each other. I'm always smoothing things out. That's one thing about Stephen that grates. He doesn't care. He just gets mad, whines, and mopes. Why do I have to always be the smiling, make-nice person? Just once, I'd love to do some of the complaining," he says.

"Consider this: Maybe you're not such a nice guy after all," I say. "The good news is that you might discover that to be a great relief. You also might discover that telling the truth is easier than you think. It might even be a better way to avoid conflict!"

His eyebrows go up. "I have no real evidence that telling the truth avoids conflict," he says.

"It works like this," I tell him. "When you are clear about what you want—as a manager, a husband, a friend—it's easier for others to accept or reject your requests. The communication is clean. There's no confusion or misinterpretation."

Daniel weighs my words, and looks silently out the window again.

"This is new territory. It will take some practice for you to be more straightforward and direct. We'll start small, build your muscles, and see what happens," I say. "By the way, nothing is too small. Everything is an opportunity for practice."

Daniel smiles.

The light in the room is fading. Daniel is sitting
forward in his swivel chair. I can almost feel the wheels
turning in his head.

He starts slowly. "This 'nice guy' conversation has
me thinking about a situation with my wife. When I
get home from work I need about twenty minutes to
unwind, stare at the wall, read my e-mail. My wife
gets home about the same time I do. She's excited to
see me and is always full of things to say. I give her a
half smile and pretend to listen, but I'm all tied up
inside hoping she'll stop, or the phone will ring, so I
can escape and space out. I never just say to her, I need
twenty minutes. I feel like a nice guy wouldn't say that.
But I'm beginning to see it differently."

"Go home tonight and tell your wife that you
need twenty minutes. You're allowed to ask for what
you want. It doesn't guarantee that you'll get it. But
assume she has the best interest of the relationship in
mind. Assume that it never occurred to her that you
need some unwind time. You'll be educating her. Let's
practice," I say.

Daniel asks me several times, trying out different
voices and different tones.

"Madeleine," he practices, "can you just leave me
alone for a little while, just don't talk to me," he says in
a tentative, strained voice.

I suggest that he be specific, ask for twenty minutes,
tell her he needs some quiet time. I point out that
his voice sounds uncertain and suggest he try again,
assuming that Madeleine will be happy to give him his
time. He begins to get comfortable with the idea. It no

longer seems like an outrageous thing to ask for.

He calls me the next day. "Whoa, that went really well!" he says. "It turned out that I got home about an hour before Madeleine, so by the time she got home I was relaxed. It was much easier to have the conversation because I already had my time to unwind. I told her I wanted to have a little chat. I said I noticed that when I get home, I need about twenty minutes of quiet time. After I've had that time, I'm a much happier camper, I can listen to her stories, cook, clean, whatever is needed. I asked her whether she would support me in making sure I take that twenty minutes for the sake of the relationship. You know what she did? She stood up from the table and gave me a big hug! She was thrilled that I was asking for what I wanted," he says.

The phone is pressed to my ear. A big grin spreads across my face. I look out the window at the flowering pear. So much is blooming.

"What is the gift?" I ask.

"I was mad at Stephen. Not because he's late to meetings or doesn't finish his work. I was mad at him because as his manager, it was my job to confront him and tell him what I observed," Daniel says to me. "That brought me face to face with something I didn't want to see in myself—how hard it has been to tell people what I want, how hard it is to set boundaries. I have a long way to go, but I feel like I'm on my way. Thank you, Stephen!"

Podunk, Nowhere

Margaret calls me in a low-grade fury. "My husband got this new job in Podunk, Nowhere. I mean, we are in the middle of nowhere. I'm going crazy here. Todd followed me for our last move, so now it's my turn to follow him. I had a wonderful medical practice with a group of really smart, engaging women. I gave it up to come here. My marriage is important to me. I tried to figure out a way to commute, but it just didn't work. I hate this town. My people aren't here. I feel so isolated. I'm working four days a week, and I just don't know what to do with myself," she says.

Margaret is in her late fifties. She and Todd have two daughters, one a college freshman, the other a graduate. She had been a full-time mom, full-time doctor, and full-time wife for more than twenty years. Suddenly, here she is in an unfamiliar town, with no community. Her kids are out of the house, and she's working in a medical practice with a group of men who are unaccustomed to energetic, outspoken women. She is angry, frustrated, and wants things to be different. She wants me to fix it, and fix it fast.

"Margaret, this is big. Your life has been seriously shaken. Not one way, not two ways, but at least five ways. You gave up your medical practice. That, all by itself, is big. You moved from a community you loved to a town where you feel like an outsider. That also is big. Your children have grown and are on their own. Huge. You are working part time, rather than full time, in a practice that doesn't value your expertise. And you're about to turn sixty. Put all these things together, and it's no wonder you're angry, annoyed, frustrated, and sad.

"I know that you are a woman of action, but some of these changes can't be undone," I say. "Moving to Podunk, as you so affectionately call it, is not simply a variation of your previous life. It is a quantum change. Yet you are applying the same expectations, hopes, and dreams from your previous life to your Podunk life. That won't work. It's time for a new blueprint, one with new expectations and a new perspective."

Margaret's new home is on an acre of land. Long windows in every room flood the house with light and provide views into a small forest of trees that are now leafless. The winters are long, but the spring will be spectacular. The walls of her home office are filled with family photos and floor-to-ceiling bookcases. A ceramic coffee mug sits on the end table next to a high-back chair. This is where she sits when we have our conversations. She tells me that from her chair she can see the colorful bed of fall leaves moist from the recent rain.

I sense an impatience in Margaret. She's used to being in control, making things happen. She's a mover and never approaches a day without a schedule. She has a false sense that if she keeps moving, she can rearrange the pieces in a way that suits her better. Suddenly, there are too many pieces, and some of them refuse to be rearranged.

"Your children have grown and gone. They will never stop being your children, but family as you've known it is no longer. You can grieve. You can celebrate and acknowledge your role in their growth and development. But this piece in the constellation of changes cannot be altered," I say.

"I know, I know, they're gone. Yes, I miss them. But I don't think that's the really big issue. The really big issue is my work. I was in a practice with a group of women, very progressive in their thinking, and we had a strong camaraderie. These bozos here are from the Stone Age. They are patronizing old men with no regard for women. We have nothing to say to each other," she says.

"Margaret, let's look at this from another perspective," I say. "Like it or not, you have just entered a new stage of life. Maybe these bozos, to use your words, are providing just the nudge you need to reshape your life. Just as, while you will always be a mother, your responsibilities are significantly different now from when your kids were young. While you are still a doctor, maybe the nature of your practice also needs to change.

"Are you open to exploring, to taking some time to get quiet and discover what this new phase is all about? You are in a new season of life, you might even call it the Podunk season! Here you are with an opportunity to slow down and reevaluate. Tell me what that sounds like to you."

"I just feel so mad," she blurts. "I'm mad at the stupid doctors; I'm mad at this town and its provincial, limited world view; I'm mad that I had to give up my medical group. I miss my friends, I miss my kids, I feel like a stranger in my own life." She pauses for breath. "Oh, and I'm mad that I'm almost sixty, that my body doesn't do what it used to be able to do and that people call me ma'am, like I've crossed over some line. I don't want to get old and die in this place!"

"Margaret, you and Todd moved to Podunk as a kind of experiment. He had a great job offer, and you decided it was worth the risk. You and Todd didn't commit to staying forever. Are you willing to give it a shot for a year? Think of yourself as an exchange student, on sabbatical from your real life. How would you like to use your time? What would you like to learn? Academically, creatively, emotionally, spiritually? Think of it as a reprieve from the world that you have known. Engage parts of yourself that have gone unnoticed and unused. Wake up another aspect of Margaret," I say.

A soft "hmmm" comes into my ear. "I'd like to learn to slow down," she says after a pause. "You're right, I'm always on my way to someplace else. My friend Monica told me about how you and she came up with the idea of cat-in-the-sun time. I have to admit when she first said it to me, I thought, 'Why would anyone want cat-in-the-sun time? I can rest when I'm dead.' But I guess as I get a little older, as I see how quickly my kids grew up and took off, I feel as if I'm missing some things because I'm always on to the next thing. I noticed that even though I made fun of cat-in-the-sun time, I never forgot about it.

I like what you said about this being the Podunk time of my life. I don't know, something shifts if I think of this place as some bizarre opportunity. A time to go inside. Like winter."

It seems as if Margaret has let her shoulders down a few notches. Something is softening.

"I'd like to be a little less stubborn, more flexible. I walk out into the world with my dukes up, ready to take on anyone and everyone. Maybe if I weren't so ready to fight, fighting wouldn't find me so easily," Margaret says.

"In light of this being the Podunk season, how would you like to redesign your life to honor where you are, rather than rise up to fight against it? Let's evaluate your current situation. What works and what doesn't work?" I ask.

"Even when everything else is changing, two things are very central for me: community and professional collaboration," she says. "I pour myself into things. I pour myself into the people in my life and the projects I take on. You're right, the money doesn't matter right now. It's more about my self-expression. The qualities I want to develop are patience, surrender, and acceptance. Oh, and I guess vulnerability."

Our weekly calls continue for several months. During that time, she swings back and forth about whether to leave the new medical group. The physicians give her ample opportunity to practice patience and acceptance. She stops trying to change their attitudes about medicine and women, making her own life calmer. On our calls she often refers to her Podunk season.

"I can see that I'm softening, and ironically, it has

something to do with being around these rigid old docs. I'm embarrassed to admit it, but I'm starting to like a few of the old guys. I even think maybe they are starting to like me. I've never known the middle ground. I thought the middle ground was for cowards. What I see now is that middle ground might actually allow more room for change than the high road I've been staking out for so long," Margaret says.

"I think I'm afraid to stop working," she admits on one of our calls. "It surprises me to hear myself say that, but I think it's true. I wouldn't know what to do with myself. I've always worked."

"What if you worked three days a week and took two days to be on your own, take some quiet time, find out what else might interest you? This is another example of middle ground," I say.

There is a long silence on the phone. I don't say anything. Margaret is wrestling with my suggestion.

"Give me some time to think about it," she says. "It's easier to consider if I think of it as part of my Podunk season, as my time to explore and discover. Then it's not quite so scary."

After much list-making and weighing all options, Margaret decides to work three days a week and to explore some unstructured days. The transition isn't easy. She keeps reminding herself that this is a period of reevaluation and transition. She keeps her heart and mind focused on finding the middle ground in all her actions. Using those words gives her a new perspective and a greater acceptance of what life is delivering in her Podunk season.

SALLY

Hors d'Oeuvres

Sally and I have been working together for several months. She has been building the muscles that allow her to speak directly, ask for what she wants, establish boundaries, and say no when it's called for. She often comes to our call with success stories. Like a runner building endurance, each week she adds a few more miles to her training program. Her voice is stronger and clearer, her requests to the point. But she sounds less confident than usual when we speak one afternoon.

"The good news is my daughter is getting married," she says. "The bad news: My ex-husband is going to be there. This is not neutral to me. He is an unreliable human being, part liar, part snake charmer. Even when he's sober he's a tricky guy to be around. I can't even revel in my daughter's engagement because the thought of seeing him so unnerves me."

Sally is a poised woman, tall and graceful. Heads turn when she enters a room. Her presence is large and inviting; she's a natural hostess. Nothing in her bearing suggests that she would be afraid of anything. She divorced fifteen years ago, a year after the last child left home. Jim moved across the country and started a new life, so she rarely has to deal with him. Having to see him falls in the category of potential catastrophe.

"I'm going to suggest something outlandish," I say. "This is good news, really good news! In fact, this is an acknowledgment of all the work you've been doing. You are ready to see Jim. There's still work to do, some practice, but you're up for it. Think of it as an opportunity to measure how far you've come."

Sally used to think people were taking advantage of her. She'd keep her mouth shut, until she couldn't stand it anymore and then explode, way out of proportion to the situation, venting her wrath on people who didn't really deserve all that stored-up anger. But things are changing for her.

"The other day a car mechanic told me I needed new brake pads," she says "I know cars. I've grown up doing minor repairs, and I know enough to ask the right questions. I asked to see the brake pads. There was definitely wear, but not enough to put new pads in at this point. In a very calm and direct voice, without being punitive, I told him that his business is built on trust, and that it is in his best interest to tell his customers the truth. I didn't stick around to see whether anything I said made a difference. He lost my business, no need for me to give him a second chance. I didn't blow up at him. I told my truth and walked away. Oh, it felt so good."

"Bravo for you. Imagine how you would have behaved in the car mechanic situation a few months ago. Compare that to how you did react. You've taken giant strides. If I had suggested several months ago that the car mechanic situation was a gift wrapped in an unlikely package, how would you have reacted?" I ask.

"I probably would have fired you on the spot!" Her laugh is full and big. "But, like you said, that was several months ago. I see where we're going. I'm in training. To be the best human being I can be. That takes work. It takes coming up against all the places I want to stop," Sally says.

She is so courageous. She keeps going out there into the world, wide open, with a big sandwich board that says, "I'm ready, bring it on." She is an inspiration to me.

"Let's get to work," I say. "We've got a wedding and an ex-husband to focus on. We have some serious practicing to do. I can't think of a better gift to give yourself than a sense of peace and clear boundaries. This is going to be your big celebration too!

"Talk to me about how do you want to be with your ex-husband, how do you want to behave when you see him, what you want to say or not say to him. Let's get specific."

"Yes, this is good. I need to think about this beforehand when I can think clearly. If I don't, I'll end up feeling small, saying mean things in a loud voice, and throwing cake in his face," Sally says. "What I want is to be able to say hello in a removed polite way and gracefully walk away. But he's charming. He can lure me in, and before I know it my blood starts to boil and I'm acting like a stupid person. I want to keep my distance and keep remembering that I am a worthwhile human being."

Sally takes a big deep breath.

"If he makes you feel small and scared, is there

someone coming to the wedding who knows you to be strong and courageous?"

"Yes, my sister Claudia," she says. "Claudia is my rock. She sees the best in me, even when I'm being kind of stupid. I adore her."

"Good, she is your ally. Talk to me about ways she can support you in remembering who you are at your best," I say.

Sally gives a hearty laugh into the phone. "She has a way of looking me in the eye that gets me back on track. It's a look that says, all at once, 'I love you, you're about to do something stupid, don't even go there, remember there are other ways.' It brings me back very quickly."

"Talk to her. Tell her what her job is. What is her job?" I ask.

"To make sure that I thoroughly enjoy myself at my daughter's wedding. That I am beaming with pride. That my ex-husband is like a tasty, tiny hors d'oeuvre filled with ground walnuts—which I'm allergic to—so I graciously decline when the platter comes my way. When I look at him, I think with compassion of another time of my life and see how far I have come. And when I look at my sister, I am reminded how fortunate I am to have such support," she says.

It is very quiet on the phone. Something has shifted for Sally.

"Sally, the hors d'oeuvre is a great metaphor—tasty, small, unhealthy, on a platter that continues to move throughout the room. Not overwhelming, not scary. Just a bite-sized morsel. A good way to keep him in perspective. If he starts to get bigger in your mind, go back to the image of the hors d'oeuvres!"

"Davia, I don't know how the actual day of the wedding will turn out, but so much has already opened up for me. I'm not done with this guy, I may never be done with him. But just that he's gone from being a monster to an hors d'oeuvre gives me feedback about my own growth." Sally says. "Thank you for helping me see it in this way."

TAKEAWAY

Several years ago my mother and I went on a hike in the Santa Monica Mountains. It was the spring after a massive fire had scorched the hills. We were there to see the spectacular array of flowers that only bloom after a fire. Purples and yellows and reds against the charred earth.

The beauty that erupted against so much destruction played with my mind. I wanted so desperately to be able to say, this is good, this is bad. Instead I walked a trail immersed in bittersweet contradiction.

Take a peek at your own life. What are the disappointments, disasters, and tragedies? What are the flowers that bloomed from those dark places? How has that informed what came next? How has that informed who you are with others?

Chapter Seven

Keep Big Company

We want our lives to matter. We want to make a difference. It is not easy. Stretching into challenging places takes consistent commitment. Left to ourselves we too often slip, forget, back away. But when we surround ourselves with others up to something big, we can keep each other on track, remind each other of who we are at our best.

Margaret Mead, the noted anthropologist, said, "Never doubt that a small group of thoughtful, committed citizens can change the world. Indeed it is the only thing that ever has."

Whether "the world" we focus on is the planet or our own backyard, it is our community of "thoughtful, committed citizens" who hold us to account. They are our witnesses, reflecting back to us our highest dreams, encouraging us to step forward with the best we have to offer. And in turn, we are their witnesses, encouraging them to step forward with the best they have to offer.

Be up to something big. We're in this together.

Ending Hunger

I was weaned on giving back. Looking out for the underdog. Giving voice to the voiceless. Saving a world that appeared broken and damaged. It was in my bones, my DNA. I was hungry to make a difference. To be a part of something bigger than myself.

I found the perfect vehicle, an organization dedicated to ending world hunger and poverty. What could be bigger than that? We worked with the U.S. Congress, with community groups, with the media. Against all odds, Republicans and Democrats voted to include funding in the foreign aid budget for the programs we advocated. With our encouragement and support, a few members of Congress stepped forward as champions for the end of world hunger, challenging others to do the same. We made a difference. Twenty years later, international childhood deaths from hunger have decreased by a third. We began to chip away at a monumental travesty. Still a long way to go. We were warriors for the underdog, the voiceless.

As volunteers with an international organization we committed ourselves to creating a world without hunger and poverty. Almost unthinkable. It catapulted me right out of my routine life, causing me to think and act beyond my comfort level. I stretched myself to rise up to meet the vision.

My local group met three times a month to educate ourselves on the issue and plot action. We wrote letters to the newspaper, practiced calling Congress. The first time I called my congressional representative, my hand shook as I dialed. I rehearsed my little speech over and over, and still I doubted myself. Felt like I was intruding, sure that he would be too busy to listen. Who did I think I was to make this phone call? I made the call on behalf of women I'd never met, women in Bangladesh who needed fifty-dollar loans to start their own businesses. They had no formal education and could not hope to send their children to school. I never would have called a congressman to ask for something for myself, but being in the group gave me courage. I watched others make calls and write letters. And I picked up the phone.

I came to this work to help those women who needed me, people I'd never know. But something shifted. I began to see my own hunger and poverty. The hunger in my heart. In my spirit. The hunger to make my life matter. I saw how much I was hungry to live with gratitude for all things. To live with awe and wonder.

I began to see the interconnectedness of all things too. If the world needed saving, then so did I. As I fed my own hunger, my ability to nourish others expanded. And as I worked with this group toward its large vision, something happened to all of us. As we reached for something larger than ourselves, we satisfied a deep hunger.

Something else surprising happened. The faraway

women in Bangladesh didn't seem quite so far away. On a visit to Bangladesh, I saw firsthand how micro loans allowed them to start small businesses, send their children to school, eat three meals a day. They walked differently. They talked differently. They were proud. They started speaking up. And I was not so different.

MARIANNE

Green House

"Hi, I'm Marianne," a woman says in a very small voice.

We're gathered around the oval oak table for another eight-week Inner Space, Outer Space workshop. The black night is frosty outside the window. Marianne is barely visible beneath a knitted scarf wound several times around her neck, her large, wool coat still buttoned, and her brown hair coming in close around her face.

"Welcome," I say. "This workshop is for people who want to complete a big goal. Our weekly meetings provide a structure that keeps you accountable. This community will hold you to your word, expect you to give your best, and accept you as you are. Working toward a big goal is challenging. It will test you in unpredictable ways. You will discover where you get stuck, what stops you, and what frustrates you. You will come face to face with your demons. That's why it's important to be in an environment that continues to call you forward. Without the group structure, it's too easy to quit, change your mind, or disappear.

"You are in this together. You will learn from one another, and you will support one another. Sometimes you'll need specific tools, sometimes you'll want another perspective, sometimes you'll need your feet held to the fire. Each week you will choose a task, something that moves you toward your larger goal. I'll work with you to choose something tangible and specific that you can accomplish by the next class session."

Heavy coats and scarves are draped over chairs. One woman holds her mug of tea close to her face. Another doodles on her notepad. We meet in the second-floor dining room of a century-old house. The room is spare, with pine floors and pale blue walls. The oval table fills the entire room.

"I'm an architect," Marianne says. "I want to retrofit and design green houses. My own hundred-year-old house is drafty, the furnace is really inefficient, and the insulation is a joke. I have this idea that I want to green my own house and use it as a model. But I've been talking about doing it for years and haven't taken any steps toward making it happen. I'm hoping that if I come to this workshop, and surround myself with people who are also working on their own projects, that maybe, just maybe I'll get it moving."

Smart move. The other women smile and nod their heads as she talks.

We continue around the room. Each person introduces herself. Each woman has something she wants, something she hasn't been able to do on her own.

"As you report on your task, I'll use everything you say to support you in moving forward. Even when the task doesn't get completed, we'll use that as information. If you get stuck, I'll ask you questions to tease out what is stopping you. Maybe you need more information, maybe something scares or confuses you. Sometimes it's simple to untangle, sometimes more obtuse. As I focus my coaching on one person, I invite the rest of you to listen as though I'm talking to you. Sometimes it's easier to understand where you get stuck when you see it in someone else," I say.

Sonja says: "I've been spending a lot of time with my parents. I'm starting to get resentful. I want my sister to take some of the weight, but I need to ask her in a way that works. I'm looking for the right language." Everyone in the group can relate. They've all had to make tricky phone calls to relatives, friends, or co-workers. Amanda says, "I'm a poet. I have hundreds of poems that I'd like to submit for publication, but I need support with the process. Writing poetry is somehow easier for me than figuring out the submission process. I need a game plan."

And we go around the table until each of the nine women have a goal for next week.

The next week, we again go around the room, and each person checks in.

Marianne's task was to identify all the possible changes that would make her house more green. "Now that I have the big picture, I'm better able to make choices about what I want to do, by when, and what the costs will be. Even if I only do one thing on my list I'll be ahead of the game!" she told the room. "So I made my list. I discovered that it is a finite list. That feels really good. This week's task is to start researching the options. I want to get ballpark figures on costs, contact contractors for bids, learn about the payback timeline, and calculate what difference each change will make."

The nine women around the table give Marianne their full attention.

The third week, the women return. Marianne's hair is pulled back off her face. She takes her scarf and coat off and hangs them on the back of her chair. She is smiling. There is more Marianne available.

"I'm researching furnaces. My old furnace is operating at about 60 percent efficiency. I found one that has 92 percent efficiency. I'm very excited. I've spoken with three different dealers, and I'm getting a great education on what works and why. Now when I work with my clients, I'll be so much better informed and can really recommend a product that works," she says.

The other women are paying attention, wondering about their own furnaces. They come to her with their questions. They look to her for expert advice. The next week the scarf is gone, her hair still pulled away from her face, her voice clear and certain.

Each weekly check-in serves to keep everyone focused. The women ask each other how they can be supportive. They hold one another accountable. They expect the best.

The night before the fifth workshop, Marianne calls Sonja, frustrated and disappointed. She doesn't want to come to class. The house project suddenly seems too big, she didn't make any of the phone calls she said she would make, and one of her clients decided against installing solar panels. Sonja listens to all her frustrations, then she gently and insistently reminds Marianne that everyone in the group hits roadblocks. "Come to class," she says. "We need you there."

During check-in the next night, Marianne does in fact arrive. Sonja tells the group, "I felt like it was up to me to let her know how much we all need one another. We all fall down, and we're here to pick each other up. Last week it was me. I felt like I wasn't making any progress. I didn't want to come, but I did and it made such a difference. Anyone can make progress when it's easy. What matters to me is that you showed up when it's hard. Thank you, Marianne."

At the end of the eight weeks, Marianne bought a new furnace and had it installed. She got bids from three companies for insulating her walls and began to research a gray water system. She decided that the house had the wrong exposure for solar panels.

More vitally, she showed up each week, even when she didn't feel like it. She brought her failures, her vulnerability, and her successes to the group. They carried her and she them. She signed up to take the workshop again, recognizing the value of being surrounded by others who were also up to something big.

MICHAEL, DAVID, ANNIE, GEORGE, AND DEBRA

Talking About the Weather

"Davia, we want to design a project that will educate our local community about the implications and effects of climate change. Will you facilitate the process?" Michael asks me.

Michael is a geologist, familiar with the science of global warming. He wanted to take action that would make a difference. He chose to volunteer with a national nonprofit organization focused on climate sustainability. He was impressed with their clearly stated goals, strong track record of results, and unique non-adversarial change strategies.

The local chapter of the organization is ambitious and energetic. I accept Michael's invitation to facilitate a strategic planning session. I ask them questions, listen for their values, brainstorm ideas, and tease out their goals. At the end of the day, they have a design for an educational event, have identified clear goals, created a timeline for tasks, know their key players, and have set their date. We decide to meet once a month in person, once a week by telephone, and to be in regular e-mail contact until the event happens.

"Each person will walk out of here today with specific tasks. Putting on this event will stretch you," I tell them. "It will test you to your core. I know you already know this, but it bears repeating: The climate conversation is a huge issue with global implications. The playing field is already littered with 'blame and shame,' 'he said, she said,' 'mine is bigger,' 'I'm right, you're wrong' conversations. Your challenge is twofold: to carry out actions in support of the larger vision and to be a person of integrity in the process. This will not be easy. But then, you already know that. That's exactly why it's worth doing. And that's why it's so smart that you have come together, to support and expect the best from one another."

There are five people in the group. All are committed. Some are thinkers, some are doers, some are planners. Everyone will get to stretch.

Michael has a quiet manner. He's comfortable doing research and staying behind the scenes, but people make him a little nervous. He feels strongly about a climate initiative and is willing to push beyond his nervousness if it will make a difference.

"It takes my breath away, but I would like to work with our congressional offices. I know that my science-based background gives me credibility, and that goes a long way when you're trying to make a case for an issue," Michael says.

Michael, David, and Annie agree to reach out to their congressional offices. David is an architect in his early forties. He designs green buildings. He hasn't ever been part of a cause, but decides he can no longer keep quiet. His gift is his ability to see the large picture. Annie is in her midfifties and has worked on local political campaigns for a number of years. She is levelheaded, sees all sides of an issue, and freely speaks her mind. She is greatly respected by the group. Her work with political campaigns has brought her into congressional offices on many occasions. David and Michael are brand new to the activist game.

"I'm fearless when it comes to making phone calls," David says. "But my follow-through, well, let's just say, I have no follow-through. That's where I need support."

"I'm great with follow-through," Michael says. "The success of my work depends on it. We can support each other in that way. I'll help you create a system for tracking what you've promised people you'll do, and make sure it gets done. You can help me prep for calls."

Two other members of the group, George and Debra, want to contact local businesses. They decide to write a script. The first draft is an invitation to talk: "Dear Local Business Person, We're hosting an event to get our neighbors talking about climate change. We want to involve local businesses. Can we set a time to talk about how we might work together?" Drafting the script allows them to get clear about what they want from the businesses. George is a filmmaker in his late thirties. He has lived in the community his whole life and has many contacts. He is a natural connector. Debra teaches economics at the local high school. It was her students' interest in climate change that piqued her interest.

"Remember," I say, "every interaction is an opportunity to educate and create partnerships. Building relationships—that is the key. You are looking for common ground. Ask yourselves what matters to the businesses. Discover how you can help each other. This is not about asking for money; this is about expanding the width and breadth of your message. The clearer you are about what you want and why it matters, the easier it will be to invite others along."

We gather in George's dining room for our next meeting. Six mismatched chairs are pulled around a pine table. Large Post-it pages hang from the walls. Our brainstorming session is recorded in a rainbow of Sharpie colors. A water pitcher and water glasses are on the table. Each person has a pen and lined notepad. Michael's frameless glasses sit in front of him on the table. Annie is twisting her hair band around her wrist. George's chocolate Lab is asleep under the table.

"I'll call my congressional office by next week," Michael says. "We want to set a meeting with the staffer to find common ground and create an alliance. I'll talk with Annie first, so that I can practice how to say what I want to say. Yes, I'm nervous."

Annie and David agree to call their congressional offices as well. George and Debra agree that they will each contact three local businesses. We schedule a call for one week later.

"I want each person to check in, tell us what you agreed to do, what you did, what you didn't do, what worked, and what didn't work," I say on our weekly call. "We'll use everything as information to keep the process moving toward the end goal."

"I agreed to contact three local businesses and set dates for conversations." George's voice is big and animated. "Some real big surprises. I did contact three businesses and did set three dates. The surprise came when I was talking with the owner of a small boutique. Not only did she get very excited by the scope of our project, but she told me I had to speak with her neighbor, the owner of the coffeehouse. I wasn't even planning to talk to him. I don't know why, some rumor or incident made me think he would just dismiss me. Apparently, the boutique owner and the coffeehouse owner have been having conversations about how to address climate change. They are thrilled that we want to educate the community and take action. I guess what worked is that I made the contacts that I said I would, and the outcome completely exceeded my expectations."

I'm sitting at my desk with the phone pressed to my ear. A quote from Marianne Williamson's book, *A Return to Love,* on the bulletin board above my desk reads, "We were born to make manifest the glory of God that is within us. It's not just in some of us; it's in everyone. And as we let our own light shine, we unconsciously give other people permission to do the same. As we are liberated from our own fear, our presence automatically liberates others." George stepped forward. He even surprised himself. The group felt emboldened by his success.

"I didn't have such good luck," Michael says. "Annie and I met with each other. We talked about what we wanted from the congressional offices and what was the best strategy for getting it. Even as scared as I was, I felt confident making the call. I left one message, two messages, three messages, and never got a return call. It was really frustrating. I just want people to pay attention and realize just how serious this whole thing is. Why do they put their heads in the sand?"

"Michael, first of all, take a minute to acknowledge yourself," I suggest. "Have you ever done anything like this before? Have you ever contacted your member of Congress for anything? You just took a giant step. Remember this isn't only about producing the event. This is about how you behave as a human being in the process. You just demonstrated that you are a person of courage, extending yourself beyond your place of comfort, into new territory. It will feel unfamiliar. You might even call it painful. Or you could call it growing and stretching."

I've been in Michael's shoes on more than one occasion—with my trainer at the gym, speaking to a large audience, in a congressional office, writing a story. It's not easy. There is no certainty. At the gym, my body screams, "Stop, it's too hard!" In front of an audience, my mind says, "Who do you think you are anyway?" In a congressional office, I try to shut out the voice that says, "You're nobody." I appreciate his courage. I look up again at the quote, "... As we are liberated from our own fear, our presence automatically liberates others."

"Let's look at it as a scientist would," I say to Michael. "What did you observe? What worked and what didn't work?"

"I practiced with Annie," Michael says. "That went really well. I feel much clearer and stronger about what I want to say. It also worked that we set a specific time to practice. If we had left at the end of the day without a set time, I doubt we would have done it. I left a message at the congressional office. I'm not sure if that worked or didn't work, since I haven't heard anything back from the office. And I'm not sure that leaving three messages was such a good idea. Maybe now they just feel bombarded and might not call back at all. I'm not sure where to go from here."

"Thanks for breaking it down like that. Now you can see what the next steps are without so much judgment. Does anyone have any suggestions for Michael about how to make contact with the office?" I ask.

"You know," Debra says, "I just found out that my neighbor is a friend of one of the staffers. Why don't we connect with her and see how we might set up a meeting with all of us?"

"Wow!" Michael says. "That would be awesome. That's brilliant."

I continue to meet with and talk to the group over the next six months. Each time we talk I ask the same questions: What worked? What didn't? We look at where they are moving forward and where they get stuck. Sometimes it requires a little more pushing in the stuck places. Sometimes it's time to switch gears and try a different strategy.

The day of the event finally arrives. Some things work better than others. It brings together several local businesses, though not as many as hoped. Friends and neighbors show up and spend time at the various booths learning more about climate issues. The group had hoped more businesses and more community members would come, but it did create a strong relationship with the coffeehouse owner and the boutique owner, and all of them are already thinking about next year's event.

It took months of hard work. No one quit, though there were times when each team member considered it. They're all speaking to one another, though there were days when Annie gave George the silent treatment, and when Debra's temper flared. They kept coming back to the vision they had for something bigger than themselves. It steadied them, anchored them.

"I have this image of us standing in a circle, holding the edges of a trampoline, and one of us is in the center and we're holding tight as she bounces higher and higher," David says. "We are the support and the encouragement and cheering team. Each of us has bounced higher than we had any idea we could. No way we could have done this solo."

Movement and growth happened on two fronts: micro and macro. On the micro level, each group member developed new skills and attitudes. At the macro level, the call to action for climate sustainability was amplified. The climate issue was not solved, but as the group worked together toward a common goal, it set a process in motion. Nothing is linear. There is no straight path, no single end point. Growth happens in spirals and waves. It is quiet and then the unpredictable occurs.

CHARLES, MONICA, SUSAN, RAYMOND, AND WILLIAM

Embracing Fund-Raising

"I can't tell you how much I don't want to do this," Charles says to me and his fellow nonprofit board directors at our first gathering. We're in the eighth floor conference room of one director's office. It's quiet and comfortable, with a long table, white walls, carpeted floor, and a row of high windows that lets in the daylight. "I don't feel neutral about fund-raising, about asking people to part with their hard-earned money," he continues. "No, it's something I actively avoid doing. It's intrusive, inappropriate, none of my business, someone else's job, this isn't what I signed up for, and the list of reasons goes on and on."

ABC is an international child health care organization. I have been invited by the board to facilitate its fund-raising campaign. The board members, Charles, Monica, Susan, Raymond, and William, know that raising money is part of the job—a commitment they take on when they join. All of them believe deeply in the mission of the organization. When Monica invited me to work with the board, she emphasized how much they all hate their fund-raising obligation. Charles, a baby-faced high school principal with a good-natured sense of humor, is the most vocal about his feelings, but he's certainly not the only one dreading the task ahead.

"You are here today because you believe in the work of your organization," I tell the group. "Part of your role as a board member is to raise money to sustain its work. The subject of money is large and heavy and tangled and convoluted. It is important to discern your attitudes and opinions, notice whether or how they interfere with your ability to raise money, and notice how they support you in making powerful requests."

Before the meeting, I interviewed each board member over the phone. I asked questions and listened to their stories. I wanted to know what I was walking into. I also wanted them to see how gentle I could be in order to build their trust as we embark.

Charles is tapping his foot against the side of the table. Susan is drawing dollar signs all over the page. William is smiling. He was on the board last year. He feels a thousand times more confident about raising money this year. Last year's campaign gave him an opportunity to observe and examine his beliefs about giving, and this year he's excited about asking people to invest their money in something that makes a difference. This is a dramatic shift for him. He is a pediatrician, seeing patients who are generally strong and healthy. In his early thirties, he doesn't have children of his own but wants to do something for children who don't have the financial resources that his patients have.

"Before we talk about your attitudes about money, I'd like to find out why you are on the board of ABC. What inspires you to give your time and energy to this organization?" I ask.

I'm at the flip chart, recording everyone's comments.
"We have focused, goal-oriented, health care campaigns for children. We deliver. With a limited budget, we have a large impact," Raymond says.

"We create alliances with unlikely partners. I like how we reach out and build bridges," Susan says.

"We've documented that healthy children are better ready to learn," Charles says.

"We have programs targeted for young girls. Girls become women, women become mothers, mothers provide an anchor for family. Their health and well-being is essential to the health and well-being of the family," Monica says.

The flip pages are filling up. Everyone is smiling. There is a sense of pride in the room for the large vision. Each board member comes to the table with a different perspective. As I record all their comments, they begin to see the organization in a broader way, through the eyes of everyone else in the room.

"You should be proud. The board and staff are responsible for the results that you are talking about. You are part of the team that made this happen. Own it, acknowledge it. Is this an organization you would like to invest in? In addition to your time and energy, would you like to put your money toward the success of this mission?" I ask.

The question is rhetorical. All the board members make financial contributions—not because they are asked but because they believe and want to offer support.

"Imagine for a moment that other people want to feel

that same sense of pride and ownership, that they want to be part of something that makes this difference. You have the opportunity to tell them about what you do and invite them to invest their own time and money. Not everyone will want to participate, not everyone will be as excited as you are, but some will be incredibly grateful to you. Your job is to ask and ask, knowing that some will say yes and some will say no. The cleaner and clearer your request, the cleaner and clearer the response," I say.

Monica says, "I love what you're saying. You're reminding me again why I do this work. If I keep our mission and successes front and center, asking for money seems much more natural. I also realize that if someone asks me to contribute money and I feel like I have to say yes, then I get resentful, but if I feel really OK about saying no thank you, then I don't mind that I've been asked. If I'm really straightforward with my request, not begging or badgering or being apologetic, then they can respond much more easily. The more I practice asking, the better I get at it. Thanks."

I give each person a script and have them look it over and read it aloud several times. I ask for two volunteers. Susan and Raymond agree to go first. They will practice asking each other for money. I give them some direction.

"Susan, Raymond is a good friend of yours. He supports a number of child-related projects. You are excited to be able to ask him for money," I say.

"Ray, um, I have something I want to talk to you about. Something that means a lot to me. I don't know, maybe this will be interesting to you. You know I'm on the board of ABC. Well, maybe you don't know. Well, I am. How much do you know about ABC?" Susan says.

"Susan, let me pause this conversation," I say. "Tell me what's working so far and what's not working?"

"I'm tripping over my words. I'm busy in my head wondering what he's thinking," she says.

"Imagine Ray knows about ABC and he wants to give you money," I say. "What would you say then?"

"Ray, it's your lucky day. I'm raising money for ABC and I know how much you love the organization and that you want to make a contribution. How about writing us a check for $5,000?" she says. "That's pretty funny, 'cause I've never even asked anyone to give more than $500, but because you said that he's ready to give, I figured what the heck. He can always say no and then I can ask how much he'd like to give. This is bordering on being fun."

I work with the team for several hours. Everyone gets to practice with the others. I encourage them to give themselves feedback. They also get feedback from their fellow teammates. They begin to see what works and what doesn't. They notice when they founder, when they are nervous, when they tell a story that forwards the conversation. They discover that asking for money requires practice, like learning to make free throws or kick field goals. The more they practice, the more their requests are on target. When they get lost, they go back to why they do what they do, why it matters to them.

At the end of our session, each board member makes a list of fifty people, and commits to contacting each one. A goal is set for each board member to raise $5,000 within one month. This is a stretch, bigger for Charles than William, scarier for Susan than Monica and Raymond. A stretch, nonetheless, for all of them.

We set up a round-robin buddy system, and we talk together as a team once a week.

At our first call, I say, "Let's start with a check-in. Tell us how many people you've contacted, how many face-to-face meetings you've had, how much money has been committed. I also want to know what's working and what's not working."

Charles starts. "I'm not going to say this is easy, but after all the work we did last week, I know why I'm asking, and I can see where I get stuck," he says. "I called seven people, had one face-to-face meeting, and have no money committed so far. Here's what works: I assume that the people I'm about to call are waiting to hear from me, that they want to hear what I have to say, and that they are looking for a way to make a contribution. It makes me feel as if I'm in partnership with the person I'm about to call, rather than on opposite sides of the fence."

I am relieved to hear from Charles. I know that fundraising is challenging. Like a toddler learning to walk, he'll have to take a step, fall down, get up, take a step, fall down, get up. Asking for money stirs up so many conversations. Conversations such as: "There's not enough," "How intrusive to even ask," "People saying no," "People getting annoyed." We come together, so we can listen to something that will encourage us to keep going, to fall down, and get up again until we've gained our balance, our stride.

Monica has had the most experience asking for money. I'm curious to hear how her week has gone. "I can't do this anymore, it's too hard," she says. "I left messages for fifteen people. I didn't speak with one person. Why is it so much harder this year than last?" she asks in a defeated voice.

"Talk to me," I say. "Tell me about why you decided to be on this board."

"I love this work. I think ABC is a brilliant organization. I keep looking at my own kids and wondering how it would be if they didn't have health care or couldn't go to school. And then I think about the mothers who can't give their kids the care they need and it breaks my heart. I want to be every child's mother. I want all children to be safe and healthy. But I feel like I can't really make a difference. It's all too big. Yes, we do great work, but it's not enough. Asking people for money seems so futile," Monica says.

"Something needs to shift," I say. "Something is out of balance for you, and asking others for money is bringing it to the surface. Do you need to change your goal, make fewer asks, pull back on your board participation? What do you think?"

"I don't know, I just feel so tired. I've lost the spark that had me so excited about this work. It's no surprise to me that no one answered the phone; I don't want to talk to anyone! I just want to curl up with my own children and not always worry about everyone else's children," she says.

"Good, why don't you do that. What specifically

would you like to do with your children?" I ask.

"I want to have playtime with them, not always be rushing somewhere else, to this meeting or that meeting," she says.

"Will you do that?" I ask.

"Yes," she says and takes a deep breath. "Thank you. You've just relieved some of the pressure I was feeling. I may not be ready yet, but I know a couple who are very involved in international children's issues. They make large contributions to a variety of organizations, and I've been meaning to talk to them. I've even thought about inviting them to be on the board. I'd like to make a date to show them our video and ask them how they might like to become involved. Just thinking about their fresh energy makes me perk up. Charles, I think you would enjoy this couple. When I feel ready, would you come with me to talk with them?"

The group decides it wants extra support, and we increase our check-in calls to twice a week. Each week there are ups and downs, disappointments and miracles. The board members continue to support one another, and they keep at the task that's so difficult for them, asking and asking for money.

By the end of the one-month campaign, the board had raised $32,000, exceeding its goal. Monica's couple got very excited, gave $10,000 and became very involved with the organization. Monica raised another $1,500 from other donors. Everyone met (or almost met) the $5,000 goal.

"I'm still not fond of fund-raising," Charles says. "But this has been a remarkable experience. I never thought I would raise anywhere near $5,000. I'm frankly astonished. Two things made it possible. This team support experience. And constantly going back to the work we do and seeing the unbelievable impact we have had on thousands, no hundreds of thousands of children all over the world. Who wouldn't ask for money to support that?"

TAKEAWAY

Standing together we are so much bigger than when we stand alone. When we align ourselves with others equally committed, we find the will and the courage to push beyond what we think we are capable of doing, who we think we are capable of being. In community, we challenge ourselves to raise the bar on our lives.

Choose where you want to play big—whether it be in your neighborhood or the neighborhood of the world. Seek others with the same intention and come together. When you hold one another up, you can reach higher. When you hold hands, you can stretch farther.

Walls come down, attitudes shift, laws change. When we work with a shared purpose, we can move mountains.

What would you take on if you knew you had the support you needed to succeed?

Closing

A woman climbs down a steep, craggy mountain, tethered to a woman above her and a man below. Pressed against the hard rock face, several hundred feet from solid ground, all three are alert and vigilant. They are acutely aware of the rope tension, the crevices, their grip. Details are critical, attention crucial, integrity essential. Her life is in their hands.

Their lives are in hers.

The whole world is like that now, in this age of global interconnectedness. We are all tethered. We can pull one another up or we can weigh one another down. We are in it together, like it or not.

How we live matters.

Here is my invitation to you. Look beyond your personal life. Know that your movements matter, that your actions reverberate, that your words ripple across the globe. Be up to something big—by tending not just to your wildest visions but to your everyday actions. Call forth the best of yourself, and of others. Massage the fate of the world as it passes through your hands. Live as though we're counting on you to hold the rope taut.

We are.